The Complete Jogger

The Complete Jogger

Jack Batten

Harcourt Brace Jovanovich
New York and London

A Harvest Book

Printed in the United States of America

A Jonathan-James Book

(A Harvest Book)

LC 76-55527
ISBN 0-15-120699-6

First Harvest edition
A B C D E F G H I J

To the joggers and runners and researchers who showed me the way: Wendy, Tom, Chris, Sam and Reggie the Ghost.

Contents

The Complete Jogger

Prologue

"I travelled the whole world
looking for adventure, and
found it in my own body."
Dr. George Sheehan

T he humiliation arrived in
the summer of 1976. I was a mere 44 years old when, that
summer, science revealed the awful truth to me: I could not
measure up to that cliche of fitness, the 65-year-old Swede.
And it was jogging that had in a roundabout way introduced
me to this shameful fact about my body.

Like everybody who keeps an eye on trends, I was aware that
jogging had emerged in the 1970s as a movement close to
religion; and like everybody who is rapidly approaching middle age and hardly enjoying the trip, I decided that jogging
might have a message for me. I wasn't in *rotten* shape, nothing

1

that presented any immediate threat. My weight, 124 pounds on five feet six inches of small bones, matched up to the insurance company charts. I'd never smoked, and my doctor had pronounced my ticker in sound order and all organs functioning as expected. I exercised mildly, a couple of games of squash each winter week and tennis in the summer, and I kept social vices to a modest level of indulgence. I was, I summed up, fit enough for a guy in the sedentary job of writing books and magazine articles. But, I also reasoned, that wasn't good enough. I wanted to feel more exuberant. I craved health. In some small aging corner of me, I longed to experience in my heart and lungs and muscles just a whiff of the ease and energy I knew as an adolescent chasing a football pass or loping through a cross-country run. Jogging, I figured, might do the job.

But first I decided to subject myself to a fitness test, and that's when I enountered that infernally healthy Swede. I also encountered Sam. Sam had large brown eyes, a delicious little overbite and a cute figure. Sam was a girl, 20 years old, and so fit that her body seemed to give off sparks. She was a university student in kinesiology—the study of human movement—and as part of her course, she ran the fitness program at the gym where, under her guidance, I took the test that uncovered the kinks in my physical plant.

The test, which lasted an hour, was scientific stuff. Sam squeezed my body in several strategic spots with a pair of finely tuned calipers to check the amount of unnecessary body fat I was carrying around. She made me blow into a spirometer, a graded measuring device, to determine my vital capacity, which relates, roughly speaking, to my ability to take oxygen out of the air and into my lungs. She ordered me to squeeze a grip instrument that was attached to a strength indicator to test my hand and forearm muscularity. And she put me through a bunch of curious stretching postures to check my body flexibility. Those measuring devices and several others Sam inflicted on me indicated that I was average in almost everything. Average strength. Average flexibility. Average vital capacity. Slightly less than average in body fat percentage. Average pulse rate efficiency index. The last took some explanation from Sam. The index measures the number of beats my heart took per minute in order to pump blood through my system. A low score here means that the heart beats fewer times per minute, and therefore has to do less work to keep the circulatory system going. This is the mark of a healthy heart. Exercise, Sam pointed out, does wonders in lowering the pulse rate. In the meantime, I was average.

Well, average, I thought, average isn't so disastrous. Then came the bad news. The single most important test during my session with Sam took place during the six minutes I was pedaling an ergometer, a stationary bike in layman's language, while I was hooked up to an electrocardiogram machine that was assisting in the calculation of something called my Maximum Oxygen Uptake.* Oxygen, as Sam explained it, is the key to fitness, oxygen and the heart-circulatory system that moves it around the body. My muscles need oxygen as fuel to get their work done, and the more efficiently I transport oxygen-bearing blood to those muscles, the better and longer I'll be able to perform the physical tasks I face each day. As it turned out, my heart and the rest of my circulatory system weren't up to much. My score, calculated by applying the results from the ergometer test to a predetermined formula that takes into account my sex, age and weight, was 30. That's 30 milligrams of oxygen being burned by each kilogram of my body weight per minute. Thirty was a score in the middle range of fair. Thirty was below average.

What was even more devastating to me, 30 placed me somewhere to the rear of the 65-year-old Swede. Actually he was 63. His name was Bjorn Kjellstrom, the president of a company that manufactures compasses in his country, and not long before I took my test, he travelled to North America on business and stopped into a fitness center in the city where I live and put himself through a test identical to mine. What was Bjorn Kjellstrom's Maximum Oxygen Uptake? Thirty-two. Just to rub it in, he underwent the test during a period when business and travel had taken him away from his usual exercise routine. Normally his Maximum Oxygen Uptake would be closer to 35, a remarkable score for a man of his age.

*For M.O.U. chart, see page 145

Kjellstrom's secret was that all his life, like most Swedes, he had devoted himself to healthy doses of cross-country skiing and orienteering, a sport like car-rallying except that all the hurrying from point to point across the course is carried out strictly on foot. And that was a secret I wanted to get in on. Not cross-country skiing necessarily or orienteering, but some sport, calculated to nudge me closer in fitness to Kjellstrom, that would suit my personality and life style. Jogging, for example.

Sam went to work, and using the results of my fitness test as a guide to calculate the amount of exercise my body needed and could at the same time safely accept, she drew up a fitness program for me. The program was neatly plotted on a large green card for my handy reference, and it included plenty of physical odds and ends that were intended to jack up my flexibility and strength, to harden my stomach and give tone to my deltoids and triceps and my pectoralis major. As part of the program, I was to perform seated single-leg stretches and bent-knee situps and bent-over toe touches and wrist curls and roll up and tucks. However, of all of these, jogging was the most important.

"When you jog," Sam said, "you exercise almost every major body part except your stomach — and you're probably helping it, too."

Jogging would be crucial to advancing my Maximum Oxygen Uptake out of the fair category (30) and closer to average (33 to 39) or even into good (40 to 45). The relationship between oxygen and the heart and the sort of endurance training I'd get by jogging were, I learned, linked in a circular pattern. If I trained, then I would start making use of more oxygen from the air. My heart rate would drop while the volume of oxygen-bearing blood that the heart sent out with each pump would increase. Thus the blood would be carrying more oxygen and, at the same time, the muscles would take the oxygen more efficiently from the blood stream. Fascinating, I thought (especially because it was *my* fitness, *my* oxygen, *my* heart, and *my* muscles I was considering), and while Sam was preparing the training program, I ranged around in my reading at home to delve deeper into the gripping subject of *my* health. I read *Aerobics* by Dr. Kenneth Cooper and *Jogging* by Bowerman and Harris and *The Complete Runner* by the editors of *Runner's World* magazine, and I read a bunch of other authoritative volumes, not excluding one frightening but inspirational tome called *Heart Attack? Counterattack!* by Dr. Terence Kavanagh. All the books enlightened me in matters concerning my heart and my respiratory system. All fed my new fascination with my own health. And all underlined the wonders of jogging.

Sam's program, in addition to the various situps and toe touches, called for me to jog about a mile and a quarter at each exercise session. Not a straight, uninterrupted mile and a quarter, but a total of a mile and a quarter. I was to jog three or four laps on a small track (equivalent to one-eighth and one-sixth of a mile), then walk a lap to catch my breath and generally regroup, then jog again, walk, jog and so on. Two sessions like that with the other exercises performed in between would yield the mile and a quarter. Gradually, as I worked through the green card of instructions, I'd hit an even two miles after a couple of months. The increase in distance depended on the number of times I performed the program each week. Sam pointed out that I shouldn't fall below three workouts per week and that five would be more beneficial. I resolved to aim for five. Each workout, what's more, was to take place at the gym, where equipment was available for those exercises that needed it. I was to do wrist curls, for example, that required me to hold a long metal pole weighing 20 pounds in my fingers while I flexed my wrists in a particularly exotic movement. The gym, of course, was also equipped with a track. So I began my jogging program.

I won't say it was easy. In fact, I'll say that it was hard. From the outside, jogging looks like an effortless activity, feet lifting nimbly over track or over greensward, arms pumping rhythmically, body arched gracefully. Looks in this case are deceiving. Jogging, at the beginning anyway, is all about sweat and effort and pleas from the brain to please quit this nonsense.

Maybe I can best convey the emotions, not to mention the physical grind, that I went through as I started to jog by quoting some excerpts from my jogger's diary. After each day on the track, I wrote in a notebook a record of my physical, mental and spiritual reactions to the hour's workout. I tried to be honest in my jottings. I think I was. Now that I recall the agony of those first days, I probably had no choice except brutal honesty.

Day one. I experience mild pain, especially in the joints. My ligaments, so Sam says, are strained. Hence the pain as the glue sticking knees and elbows and other joints in their 44-year-old positions snaps loose. Still, I feel happy to be moving in an unaccustomed way. Euphoria sets in. The jog is fun.

Day two. Euphoria flees. I'm pinned to my bed by aches and strange twinges, particularly in the legs. I rise and move gingerly through the morning until my afternoon workout. Still, a sense of virtue fills me—how pleased I am with myself—as I finish my program for the second consecutive day. I stand under the shower and the water sprays me with tiny pellets of praise.

Day ten. Disillusionment. My body is screaming with small pains spread over its length and breadth. And a touch of disappointment is nuzzling at the rear of my mind. Is all this effort worth anything? Am I nuts to try? I tell myself not to expect improvement too soon. I must be patient. I must groove on fitness as a gradual process.

Day 14. A curious reaction seems to be occurring. As exercise time draws near, 30 minutes or so before I'm due to hit the track, nervousness begins to seep into my head and guts, and by the time I'm climbing the stairs from the locker room to the gym, I'm in a state close to panic. What is it? A psychological quirk? The body rebelling at the prospect of tough exercise after a quarter-century of relative sloth? Whatever it is, I trust I'll lick the strange obstacle.

Day 17. I note that there's a pecking order in the gym. At the top are the muscular guys who work the punching bags, lift formidable weights, whip through complex calisthenics. Even though I can't imagine that their muscle-inducing carryings-on are doing much for the old heart-respiratory system, they seem to sneer at guys like me who are grinding out the laps on the track. At the bottom of the pecking order come the portly chaps who stagger from exercise to exercise carrying their green cards like Linus blankets. I'm not sure how many rungs I rate over the portly fellows. Not many I fear. Some of them, dammit, jog faster than I do.

Day 20. Saw a kid today, maybe ten years old, a boy, running across the park three blocks from my house. He was just running. Not chasing a ball or rushing because he was it in a game of tag. He was running for the sake of running, and he looked so easy in his stride, so relaxed, as if he could run forever. He made running look like second nature. I thought of how I feel on the track, laboring even after three weeks, and I loathed the little kid. Running, I guess, is something that 44-year-olds have to relearn.

Day 25. My heart sank at the prospect of working out this morning, the thought of inflicting my body with those torture instruments in the gym. To my fevered mind, the track itself, that innocent arrangement of sloping boards, took on the trappings of an evil force. It is, of course, all in the mind. My body can stand the strain—can't it?—but my brain still has a way to go. The psychology of fitness—maybe *that's* the fly in the ointment.

Day 31. Sam says, hang in there.

But should I?

I considered throwing in the towel. Progress, if I dare to invoke such a presumptuous word, was arriving with a frustrating lack of haste. I thought of the time my five-a-week sessions at the track were eating up — the drive to the gym, quick change, 50 minutes working out, slow cool down and shower and the drive back to the typewriter, altogether consuming about 90 minutes — and then I thought of other activities I could be devoting that hour and a half to, reading books, quaffing beer, listening to Miles Davis records. I wondered whether I was making a sensible disposition of my time. Was jogging worth the effort? Would it pay off in health and pleasure and exuberance? Would I even *know* when it started to pay off? I began to wonder ...

The First Jogger

Did someone invent jogging? Who?
How did it spread to the millions who
have taken it up in the 1970s?
Here is jogging's history,
a look at its heroes and an analysis
of its remarkable impact
on hearts and health.

There wasn't as much running or jogging as you might expect in the original Olympic Games. We are talking of 776 B.C. when the first Olympics took place in a meadow beside the river Alpheus at Olympia in southwest Greece. Young Greek lads gathered there to contest events of athletic skill, boxing, wrestling, discus throwing, chariot racing, not to forget the pancratium, a combination of boxing and wrestling that cost many competitors their lives. But, comparatively speaking, they hardly ran at all, True enough, Coroebus, a youth from Elis, is generally accepted as the first winner of a laurel wreath at the first Olympics, and his event was the foot race. How far did he run? A mere 200 yards, the length of the athletic ground at Olympia. This 200-yard sprint was the only track event on the first Olympic program, and the evidence indicates that young Greeks weren't keen on long-distance running.

This fact may help to account for the death of Pheidippides 286 years later. Pheidippides was a foot soldier in the Greek army that Miltiades gathered in 490 B.C. to battle the Persian invaders "where the mountains look on Marathon and Marathon looks on the sea." Miltiades' forces, 9,000 Athenians and another 1,000 allies, were small potatoes compared with the mighty Persian horde, but they compensated for numbers with their patriotism and their fury, and they forced the Persians, howling in retreat, into the sea. Athens' elders, meanwhile, waited in despair back at the city marketplace for the expected word of their enslavement to the Persians. Not wanting to hold them in suspense, Miltiades summoned Pheidippides, who enjoyed a reputation as a swift fellow afoot, and ordered him to run the good word to Athens. Pheidippides shed his shield, his armor and his fatigue and set out the eight leagues, about 40 kilometers, up and down hill and across plain, from Marathon to Athens. He rushed within the shadow of the Acropolis, gasped his message — "Rejoice! We conquer!" — and fell dead at the feet of the elders. Very few runners or joggers have been called on to cover forty kilometers after fighting a battle to defend their homeland, there's that to be said for Pheidippides. But the question his death leaves unanswered to jogging purists is this: was the Greek running program up to scratch in training its young adherents?

Certainly the marathon was never an event in the Greek Olympics, and for the most part, running continued to take second place to other contests as the Games continued through the centuries. The passing years were, alas, mostly downhill for the Olympics. At the 98th Games, a boxer named Eupolus of Thessaly was found to have bribed three opponents to throw their fights to him. Scandal! And not the last. Commercialism set in too and competitors refused the traditional laurel wreaths, demanding cash prizes. The embarrassing Emperor Nero of Rome arrived at one Games as a competitor and stayed to build a house next door to the Olympic hippodrome. Greece fell on sad days in the world of power and politics, Rome took over, and the Games plunged into further disrepute until the decree of Emperor Theodosius I of Rome ended them in 394 A.D. All that remained was for the barbarian invaders to pillage the grand Olympic temples. By 426 A.D. they had completed the job.

Jogging in Modern Times

Over the next few centuries, nobody ran much for fun or profit unless fleeing a sheriff or a robber, and the Dark Ages, Middle Ages, Reformation, Industrial Revolution and Early Victorian times had flashed by before Baron Pierre de Coubertin got around to moving athletics once more to center stage in the civilized world. Baron de Coubertin, born in Paris in 1862, a student of political science and of education and a tireless traveler, masterminded a revival of the Olympic Games in the belief that combining education and athletics would help promote international amity. He succeeded in staging the first modern Olympics in 1896 on the outskirts of Athens, and it was here that running in general and the marathon in particular gained the popularity and admiration they have retained more or less to this day.

The marathon, that classic monument to running, was first competed for in 1896 over the same course that Pheidippides had covered centuries earlier — or as close to it as historians could figure out. Twenty-five men lined up in Marathon, and when Colonel M. Papadiamantopoulos of the Greek army fired the starting gun, they hied off for Athens. A Frenchman named Lemursiaux held the early lead, at least as far as the village of Pikermi, where citizens broke through the line of soldiers who patrolled almost the entire length of the race to crown Lemursiaux with a laurel wreath. The crowning was premature. Lemursiaux yielded the lead to Arthur Blake of Boston. It was Blake's first long run, a fact that was underlined when he collapsed at about the 19-mile mark. Then — a miracle to the Greeks! — Spiridon Loues, a skinny shepherd from the hills not far outside Athens, took first place. He retained it into the spanking new Olympic stadium, and as he entered, the Princes Constantine and George of Greece leaped from the royal box and ran alongside Loues to the final tape. It was a grand day for the homeland. An Athenian barber offered Loues free services for the rest of his — the barber's — life, so did a local tailor and a local restaurateur, and the Games concluded with Greece glorying in pride and with running back on the map.

Great long-distance runners have turned up in Olympic years throughout the twentieth century — and in non-Olympic years for that matter. There was Tom Longboat, the Canadian Indian who prospered until a training diet of whiskey and cigars took its toll. There was Johnny Hayes, a cheery New York City department store clerk who won the 1908 Olympic marathon only after Dorando Pietri, an Italian candy-maker and the first man across the finish line, was ruled to have got there on the assisting arms of several less-than-impartial officials. 1908 also saw the marathon stretched from 40 kilometers to its present official distance, 42.195 kilometers or 26 miles, 385 yards, at the whim of the British Royal family. London played host to the 1908 Games, and someone, perhaps Edward VII himself, thought it would be a treat for the monarch's young relations to watch the start of the marathon from Windsor Castle. Arrangements were carried out accordingly, and when the Prince of Wales signalled the beginning of the race, to the accompaniment of many regal whoops and hollers, the only possible route from the Castle past Stoke Poges and Wormwood Scrubs to the stadium at Shepherd's Bush exceeded the traditional 40 kilometers. So, out with the old, in with the new, and the marathon is now 42.195 kilometers.

Other great marathoners? Albin Steenroos, a 40-year-old sewing-machine salesman who won the 1924 marathon at the Paris Olympics competing for Finland as a teammate of Paavo Nurmi, not exactly a slouch himself at distance running and the winner in the 1924 Games of the 1,500 meter , the 5,000 meter and the 10,000-meter cross country. Then there came Kitei Son, 21 years old, born in Korea and a student at a university in Tokyo, who emerged from out of nowhere to trot over the macadam roads of Berlin and its suburbs and finish first in the marathon of the 1936 Games. And who could forget Emil Zatopek? He was a Czech army officer, apparently invincible, who at the 1952 Olympics won the 5,000 meters, the 10,000 meters and the marathon in the space of two weeks. "The marathon," he said later, "is a very boring race." Later appeared the African runners, Alain Mimoun, the Algerian who won at the 1956 Games, Ethiopia's Abebe Bikila, winner in 1960 and 1964, and Mamo Wolde, another Ethiopian who took the 1968 marathon, thus establishing that excellence in long-distance running wasn't the exclusive property of any continent. Frank Shorter won in 1972, the first American to finish first since Johnny Hayes in 1908, and he came second at the next Olympics, in 1976, when an East German, Waldemar Cierpinski, was the victor.

So it went down the years, men who found the nerve and muscle to run impressive distances. They performed remarkably, and for their feats, they became heroes. And that, in a real sense, was the trouble. Running, especially distance running, remained an elite activity. Champion runners made their marks and in most cities and towns around the world, there was perhaps another handful of men, often regarded as eccentrics, who ran for fun and health. Such a rare fellow was Clarence DeMar, a New Englander, a newspaper proofreader, small farmer, teacher and runner. He took part in 34 Boston Marathons and won seven of them. He ran in a ten-mile race when he was 69. But there were very few men like Clarence DeMar, and the profits of running were still confined to a minority. It was almost as if those who ran were trying to keep their activity a secret from the rest of the population that was happily going to seed.

The point, as a few pioneering souls began to realize in the second half of the twentieth century, wasn't that every man should imitate the great marathoners. The point was to absorb the most basic lesson from the marathon men: that running is good for you, that running leads to healthier hearts and bodies, that running shouldn't be confined to any one group. Marathoners stood at the pinnacle, but ordinary men could share in the inspiration they offered. A marathon, it's been pointed out by Russ Harris, director of the Aerobics Activity Center of Dallas, "is about 20 miles further than anyone has to run to get to an optimum health benefit." Every man couldn't be a Clarence DeMar—and doesn't have to be—but every man might profit from his example.

That was the message a few men set out to preach in the 1950s and 1960s. Seymour Lieberman, for one, began to practice a kind of slow running in 1953. He was 45 at the time, an attorney in Houston, Texas, who was unnerved by the rapid rate at which his friends were dropping dead from heart attacks.

His slow running brought him new pep and health, and he rushed to spread the good word. Not many people listened, not at first, but he persisted, and 20 years later, the International Council of Sport and Physical Education presented Seymour Lieberman with a certificate that declared him to be the founder of the jogging movement.

Others preached the running and jogging gospel, men who were more influential than Lieberman over the long haul. Arthur Lydiard was one, maybe jogging's true inventor. Bill Bowerman was another, the man who caught the notion from Lydiard. And then the noisiest proselytizer of them all, Dr. Kenneth Cooper. By the mid-1970s these men, with their vision and persistence, had brought running to a new audience, beyond the elite and out to the masses — or at least to those who had the good sense to pay attention.

Jogging's Frontrunners: Lydiard and Bowerman

In 1962, Bill Bowerman, the track coach at the University of Oregon, took his world-record-holding four-mile relay team on a tour of New Zealand. Inevitably he got together with Arthur Lydiard, who coached New Zealand's Olympic track team and who was responsible for bringing along such running marvels as Peter Snell, one-time world champion at 800 and 1,500 meters. Bowerman was 50 at the time and apparently in good physical shape and later he described what, among other events, grew out of his visit with Lydiard:

"Arthur asked me if I'd like to go out with him and his group for an early run. So I followed him for a while, trotting along easily enough. But we kept on trotting and trotting and trotting and by the time we went six miles, my tongue was hanging out and I was ready to cash it in. Then we hit the hills. By now I was barely walking. An 80-year-old man came past me and said, 'Come on laddie, you're flagging'."

Bowerman had experienced his first taste of jogging. It was an activity that Lydiard had conceived a few years earlier to accommodate some of his former competitive runners who were reluctant to surrender the companionship and the high degree of fitness they'd grown attached to during their track years. Lydiard suggested that slow, steady cross-country runs — jogs — might be the answer. He turned out to be right and before long, the activity spread beyond his runners to many members of the local community.

Impressed with Lydiard's success, Bowerman took the new concept of jogging back to his home town, Eugene, Oregon. Bowerman had a small advantage because Eugene, thanks to the successes of Oregon University's track team, was already running-conscious. But he could hardly have expected the swarms of eager acolytes that surrounded him when he introduced jogging through lectures, the press and through his own example. Thousands of fitness-craving men and women swooped down on Bowerman's newfangled notion as the answer to their problem and by 1975, 10,000 out of the community's population of 90,000 would be confirmed joggers. As jogging's popularity spread to other centers, Bowerman realized he had an authentic Cause on his hands.

His response was to write a book. It was called simply *Jogging*, published in 1967 and co-authored by a cardiologist named Dr. W.E. Harris. Both applied their disciplines — track for Bowerman, heart medicine for Harris — and devised a system of jogging programs that would benefit any man or woman at any level of fitness from sound to dismal. Their book asked each reader to assess his or her physical condition, with the guidance of a doctor's checkup, and then to adopt one of three plans documented by Bowerman and Harris. The plans were for those in average condition (about 80 percent of the men and 60 percent of the women), for those below average (more women than men) and for those above average (more men than women). Then, within each plan, Bowerman and Harris advocated the key principle of gradualism. A new jogger, according to instructions in the book, was hardly equipped to dash off one mile on the first day. Break in gradually. That was the secret. "Consider," Bowerman and Harris wrote, "that you are in training to develop a habit of permanent, moderate exercise." Thus, for example, the book advised those in average condition to begin with a jog of 55 or 110 yards followed by a walk of the same length, the double process repeated 16 times at a pace of about one minute for every 110 yards. Follow such a schedule on Monday, Wednesday and Friday with brisk ten-minute walks and some light stretching exercises on the days in between. Gradually, by increasing the dosage each week, a beginning jogger would cover a distance through combined jogging and walking of two and a half miles three days per week, after twelve weeks of dedication to the program.

Bowerman and Harris offered no shortcuts and no promises that the jogging route to fitness would be painless, but they presented an approach that was steady and sensible. They took the element of fear out of covering long distances on foot. "Train," Bowerman and Harris advised, "don't strain." And hundreds of joggers were grateful.

Dr. Kenneth Cooper and Aerobics

A former Eagle Scout. Devout Baptist. Career air force officer. That's Dr. Kenneth Cooper, and those credentials indicate one of the two instruments of attack he brought to fitness — evangelistic zeal. The other weapon was a scientist's restless curiosity. With this combination, Cooper concocted a conditioning system and gave it a catchall descriptive: aerobics. What exactly does aerobics mean? Cooper's definition: "Promoting the supply and use of oxygen." The aim of the Cooper system is to exercise in ways that will make the body demand oxygen and circulate it in rich, efficient, thorough supply. Cooper developed his ideas on exercise during his air force years, and he spread them to a larger audience when he began publishing his books in 1968, first *Aerobics*, then *The New Aerobics* and finally, with his wife Millie, *Aerobics For Women*. The books went through several printings, sold hundreds of thousands of copies and made aerobics a seminal word in the language of fitness. The term lives on in a couple of institutions, too, the Aerobics Activity Center and the Institute for Aerobic Research, which Cooper founded in Dallas, Texas, in 1970 when he left the air force and set out to put aerobics on an unassailable scientific basis.

At the core of Cooper's system for home joggers is a 12-minute test. How much territory can you cover — running, walking or stumbling — in 12 minutes?

The result, when matched up against charts devised after lengthy analysis in the Cooper laboratory will reveal the level of fitness you are presently at. This level will in turn dictate which of Cooper's meticulously calculated exercise programs you should pursue. An example: suppose you cover from 1.25 to 1.49 miles in 12 minutes. That puts you in Category III which is Fair. Thus, you commence in the first week of your program by walking one mile in about 12 minutes and 45 seconds. Do it five times in the week. Then, in week two, cover the mile in a flat 11 minutes, a pace that will lift you slightly past a walk into a gentle jog. By week three, you'll be down to 10.30 minutes for the mile, five times per week. At week seven, you'll be handling a mile in 8:30 minutes three times in the week and a mile and a half in 14 minutes on the other two days. By the end of the program, which brings you to week ten, you'll be taking on a mile and a half in 11:55 minutes twice a week and two miles in 17 minutes on two other days.

End of phase one in Cooper's program. Phase two moves you to another chart and into the heart of the Cooper Point System, which is designed to maintain the level of fitness you've achieved in the break-in ten-week program. Cooper preaches that, as an adherent of his system, you must earn 30 points per week, preferably accumulated at the rate of five points a day over six days. How do you manage such a feat, you who were once classified as merely Fair in the twelve-minute test? Easy, You can, for instance, run two and a half miles in between 30 and 35 minutes. That earns you five points. Do it six times over seven days and you've got your 30 points for the week. Congratulations. You ought to be fit on the Cooper scale.

Cooper, it should be noted, doesn't demand that you win your points through running and jogging. His system permits points to be scored in a variety of physical activities, swimming, cycling, walking, even handball, squash and basketball. But he leaves no doubt that he rates running as the blue-ribbon event. "If you were to ask me, finally, what exercise can be used most effectively," he writes, "I'd have no hesitancy about recommending running. As one of my runners put it, 'It's like a dry martini. You get more for your money — and quicker!'"

Hundreds of thousands of men and women have gone for Cooper's martini, and it's not hard to figure out why. His system is documented. Take a test. Follow a program. Refer to charts. Go. It may occasionally be a struggle out on the road, chalking up aerobic points, but every subscriber to the Cooper system carries the blissful assurance in his heart that something close to science has proved he's on the right track.

Jogging's Critics

"One thing I really hate," Richard Nixon told the US Sports Advisory Council midway through his presidency, "is exercise for exercise's sake."

If Watergate hadn't got Richard Nixon, then joggers might have. But Nixon wasn't alone in knocking jogging. Critics have inevitably appeared, many of them medical men, who regard jogging as less than beneficial. Typically, a doctor named J.E. Schmidt wrote a short article for *Playboy* magazine in the spring of 1976 in which he revealed that jogging, while it's okay for developing "a tanned, outdoorsy look," is detrimental to the sacroiliac joints, leg veins, and, in the case of women joggers, the uterus and breasts.

Meyer Friedman and Ray Rosenbaum, two San Francisco cardiologists, parked themselves in the Nixon-Schmidt camp with their 1974 book, *Type A Behavior and Your Heart.* The doctors divided mankind into two personality groups, Type A (competitive, impatient) and Type B (phlegmatic, easygoing) and disclosed, unsurprisingly, that Type As are candidates for trouble with the old ticker. What should they do about the potential trouble? Nothing strenuous, say Friedman and Rosenbaum, nothing much beyond "walking on the flat, up very gentle hills, up one flight of stairs ... golfing, bicycling, tennis (but only doubles and preferably mixed doubles) fishing, croquet billiards ... "

What about jogging?

"Jogging," according to Friedman and Rosenbaum, "is a form of exercise in which man transforms himself into a machine. Chug-chug-chugging along, looking neither to the right nor left, panting, the man machine chugs along. And what is its goal? To see if it can chug-chug faster today than yesterday. And what is its only joy? The soothing, miraculous feeling of relief when the chug-chugging is finished."

There are a couple of ways for jogging enthusiasts to reply to such critics. One is to strike back. "The plain fact," says Dr. Terence Kavanagh, Medical Director of the Toronto Rehabilitation Centre and a pioneer in using endurance running for post-heart-attack patients, "is that most physicians have not been trained to prescribe exercise."

That's one reply. The other is to point at jogging's success stories, at all those subscribers to Bowerman and Harris and Cooper, at anyone who jogs, in a program or on his own, and who feels lighter, healthier, more rambunctious in body and mind. Will this jogger live longer than his non-jogging pals? No one can say, but the jogger will probably tell you that, for now, he's enjoying life no matter how long it lasts, more than he enjoyed it in his sedentary years.

There's a note of caution in such a reply. How come? Well, running and jogging are hardly exact sciences. Kenneth Cooper may eventually correct that situation, but joggers in the meantime ought to retain a small cautionary voice in some corner of their jogging minds. Nothing's been proven beyond doubt. Of course, Cooper makes sense when he explains the need to move oxygen to every nook and cranny of the body. Sure, Dr. Terence Kanvanagh has worked small wonders with his heart-attack victims in running programs. And, yes, every dedicated jogger will explain that the world has taken on new and vivid meaning since he started trotting a mile or so every day. But, for all the evidence, the best attitude may be the one expressed by a rich, smart, slightly cynical Texan named Grant Fitts. Mr. Fitts was 56 in 1974 when he spoke the lines that follow. He was chairman of the board of a company with assets around $800 million and he was a jogger at the Aerobics Activity Center in Dallas. Eight minutes a mile for Fitts. Not bad at all. And this, talking in his colloquial style, is what he told a *Sports Illustrated* reporter:

"My own doctor slights old Cupper. These doctors are all jealous of course. Seems the American Medical Association frowns on this exercise kick because no one yet has come up with real, hard proof that it prevents disease. And I'll agree that right now it depends on faith. But there are a hell of a lot of us who don't enjoy runnin' all that much but who suspect there's somethin' to it."

Jogging Takes Over

Critics may have raised their voices, but men and women kept on jogging and running through the 1970s in mushrooming numbers. They turned up all over the place. By 1976 there were 2,180 entrants grinding through the Boston Marathon, up from 600 in 1968. The National Jogging Association opened in 1968 in Washington, D.C., promising a jogging tip sheet to members in return for a $15 fee, and in 1976, membership swelled past 15,000. *Runner's World*, a magazine aimed at the amateurs in the running-jogging game, started publishing in 1965. Circulation was modest in the early years, a discouraging 2,000 per issue in 1970, but as the mid-seventies whizzed by, the magazine was selling 50,000 copies with each issue and subscriptions were on a steep rise.

It's impossible to estimate how many joggers emerged onto the streets and hills and tracks in the years Bowerman, Cooper and the rest began to preach their word. But it is easy enough, by reading the short articles in the back pages of newspapers and magazines in the 1970s to judge that they've been spreading in a rush of hundreds of thousands. Those stories also indicate that some of the joggers are bears for punishment. Either that or just a little eccentric.

Item: September 1973. A young man, beginning on July 1 and finishing September 7, jogged 1,750 miles from the Mexican border to the Canadian border up the Pacific coast.

Item: May 1974. Philippe Latulippe, a chief warrant officer in the Canadian Armed Forces, jogged 100 miles on a quarter-mile track in a single day. He said he never felt better. Chief Warrant Officer Latulippe was 55 years old.

Item: April 1975. The American Medical Joggers Association, an organization of 800 doctors, held a meeting in Boston. Several members presented papers on the relationship between jogging and sound health. Next day, most members went into the streets and ran the Boston Marathon.

Item: September 1976. Carallyn Bowes jogged an average of 28 miles per day for 133 days in covering 3,841 miles across the width of North America. Miss Bowes, 23, said she lost 15 pounds during the long jog and was glad to see them go.

Item: September 1976: Mabel Weeks, age 69, of Toronto reported that her purse containing $25 in cash was snatched from her hand. The snatcher, she told police was a young jogger in a red track suit. "He grabbed my purse," she said, "and kept right on running."

A jogging *robber?* If the criminal element was getting into jogging, then it was clearly an exercise that was here to stay. Every variety of man and woman jogged and ran. It was as if, simultaneously, large numbers of people had discovered the secrets that marathoners and other long-distance runners had known for many years. Now everybody was getting in on the act — and on the benefits.

"It all came about when I was about 45," one dedicated runner has explained, Dr. George Sheehan, a cardiologist from Red Bank, New Jersey, who is a student of the physiology of running. "I was following a preordained life. Very dull, stultifying. I was a seriously considering becoming a real estate agent or something interesting like that. I'd completely blown my mind. I'd fall asleep in front of the TV, get bombed out on the weekend. I was developing fat in my body, fat in my brain and fat in my soul. Then I started running. Now I'm more interested in things. It's changed my point of view. I'm more alive. Life has become a really great day-to-day enjoyment, a puzzle. I find myself trying to live each day as if it were my last. Before I wasn't playing. I wasn't having any fun. Life has become a fantastic game.''

What Is Jogging?

But, wait a minute, what *is* jogging anyway? Where did the word come from? What does it mean? And how is jogging different from running?

Shakespeare probably used it first. *The Winter's Tale*, Act four, scene three, line 74:

"Jog on, jog on the footpath way,
    And merrily hent the stile-a:
A merry heart goes all the day,
    Your sad tires in a mile-a.''

The Bard of Avon was clearly on to a significant concept — note the "merry heart" going "all the day."

But it wasn't until Bill Bowerman got down to business that anyone followed up Shakespeare's implied definition. In his book with Dr. Harris, Bowerman defined jogging as "a steady or an easy-paced run alternating with breath-catching periods of walking" or "a slow regular trot" or "the next step up from walking."

Not too specific perhaps, but at least we're circling in on the target. The basic idea is to separate jogging from walking on the one hand and running on the other. Time is the main criterion. Cooper, who appears to merge walking into running and blurs jogging in the process, allows in one of his programs for a 12-minute walk (which carried out at such a pace over three miles on five days of the week will earn 30 points). This amounts to a brisk walk and might almost be considered a jog.

Dr. Terence Kavanagh, on the other hand, declares that for his post-cardic patients, "jogging means running a pace of ten minutes per mile or slower." Numbers, numbers. Other exercise experts insist that jogging ends and running starts at the eight-minute mark.

Maybe the idea is to resist definitions. Jogging or running, the essence of the matter is to get out on the road or the track or the country lane and move the feet. A theme throughout the writings of many running-jogging advocates is that progress comes at whatever speed benefits the individual jogger-runner. With many men and women who hang in at a program, the pace will inevitably merge gracefully and imperceptibly from a jog into a run, no matter how each category is described. They jog, and in doing so, they become fit enough to run. As their legs grow stronger and oxygen uptake more productive, they find simultaneously the need as well as the means to move faster or to move further or to do both. Are they jogging? Are they running? Well, hell, they're moving. Perhaps, out of all this confusion, we should accept the definition offered by George Hirsch, publisher of *New Times* magazine in New York City and a self-described "strict amateur" at running. He once spoke of jogging in this way: "A self-sufficient, bio-degradable, Zen-tinted, non-competitive athletic which a whole nation can enjoy."

Anybody would settle for that.

Dos and Don'ts

*Train, don't strain.
*Practice LSD: long, slow distance.
*Let progress come at your own pace.

Equipping the Complete Jogger

The first question is simple.
To jog or not to jog? The second
may be tougher than you think.
What equipment should a jogger have?
Shoes, but what kind? Socks,
but what color? A notebook,
but why? This chapter gets
down to the answers.

Frank Shorter, the splendid US distance runner, says he has a preference for shoes that are light, shoes with thin soles. Desmond O'Neill, a California lawyer who competes in marathons, writes that "Commonsense tells a runner to wear solidly built (and therefore heavy) shoes when he's going long and slow distances."

Those two contradictory bits of information illustrate the problem. Shoes — and other pieces of a runner-jogger's equipment—may be largely matters of idiosyncrasy. Whatever fits and works for Jogger A may torment Jogger B. Abebe Bikila won the 1960 Olympic marathon running over the cobble-

stone streets of Rome in his bare feet. However, few joggers
outside of Ethiopia would opt for barefoot chic. They've got to
buy running shoes. Not to mention socks, shorts, jockstraps
and other odds and ends. And they must be certain their
purchases are right . Right, that is to say, for *them* . A wrong buy
could lead to pain and discouragement, and could influence
the would-be jogger to abandon jogging as a misguided piece
of business before he takes the first crucial step out the front
door.

Shoes: First and Last

In the mid-1960s, two brothers in West Germany launched a
couple of footwear companies, Adidas and Puma, whose track
shoes soon became not merely a piece of footwear but a
symbol, a sign of exercise chic. By 1976, the two companies
together with Japan's Tiger and some smaller outfits had
cornered 60 percent of the North American market in running
shoes. It didn't help the two biggest US manufacturers, Con-
verse (owned by Eltra Corporation) and Pro-Ked (owned by
Uniroyal), when President Gerald Ford rejected tariffs and
quotas in April 1976 that might have provided an umbrella
protection for the American producers. Pro-Keds suffered at
the same time from a strike among its rubber workers. Still,
there remained such a booming market around the world that
no track shoe manufacturer would be left out in the cold for
long.

Shoes constitute the jogger's single most essential pur-
chase. "Take good care of your feet," Desmond O'Neill, the
California lawyer-runner, advises. "Avoid trouble there, and
the rest of your body will get along quite well. Hurt a foot and
expect to hurt a lot more besides." A proper pair of shoes is
obviously the first line of defence, but "proper" takes in a lot of
territory. When you buy your first pair of track shoes, keep in
mind the following checklist of features.

Price : Expect to pay in the neighborhood of $25 and rising.
Sure, bargain specials abound — $9.98 for a pair of swifties —
but a few miles down the road, your aching feet won't thank

you for the money saved. On the other hand, don't fall for shoes that hint at unnecessary extras; those little strips of leather on top may look adorable, but will they help you cover the miles? Probably not. Lay out the top dollar you can afford without blowing the whole bank account.

Last : That's the shape of the bottom of the shoe, the part that's next to the sole of your foot. The two should coincide, the shape of your foot and the shape of your shoe. Check the last with your eye. Does it look straight? Then it's all wrong. It'll almost certainly squeeze your big toe out of its natural position. If you're nervy enough, you can assist the eye in its examination of the last by taking along a pencil and a large sheet of paper. Trace an outline of your foot on the paper. Now trace an outline of the shoe you've selected. Do they appear to match? No? Then choose another shoe till you've got a pair that passes the eye test.

Now for the feel test. Put the shoe on. Check to be sure that the last conforms naturally to your foot. No forcing, no pushing or squeezing. Natural conformation. Pay attention to your toes. Are they pushing past the end of the last? Or falling an uncomfortable distance short of the end? No good. Try again and again until you've arrived at the last that best suits your foot shape.

Heel : A large percentage of your jogging weight will probably land on the four or five square inches of your heel surface. Think of the shock. Think of the protection you'll need from the heel of your shoe.

Sponge rubber for heel and sole is probably a bad idea. It's too soft, and doesn't provide enough shock resistance. Hard nylon and high-density rubber go too far the other way, acting as a conveyor of shock, shooting it from heel to head. One answer: get a shoe that combines two sorts of rubber—sponge for shock absorption and high-density for stability. Crepe soles will also do the job for the heel, and so, according to some joggers, will gum rubber. Look for track shoes that are no lower in the heel than in your civilian walking-around shoes. Otherwise, you'll put extra strain on your Achilles tendon. Make sure, though, that the heel isn't so high that it tends to throw your weight forward to an awkward degree.

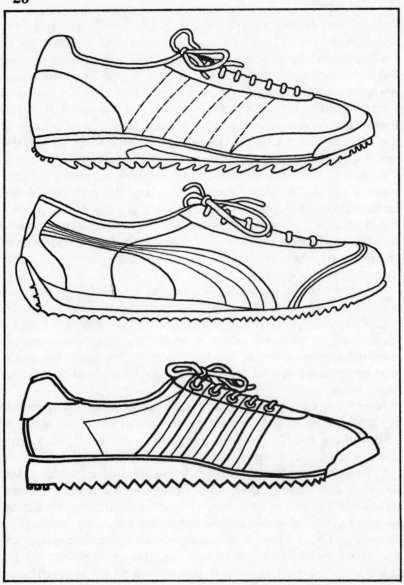

Three styles of jogging footwear

The heel of the shoe you choose must have a counter. That's a sort of cup that holds the heel in a firm but not fatal embrace and prevents it from wobbling around on the road or track. Check the counter for strength and rigidity—it needs plenty of both. Some shoes come equipped with a special container fitted into the heel, made of reinforced leather or of rubber, for extra support and protection.

Pay attention to the extension that runs from the heel up and over the Achilles tendon. It acts as extra support, but it isn't supposed to bite into your heel or tendon. Test it for fit and friction. The first should be gentle and the second non-existent.

Fit : When you try on the shoes in the store, wear the socks you'll wear in action. If you plan to use two pairs, one thin and one thicker, then take along two pairs to the store. Be prepared.

Before slipping into the shoes, give them a flexibility test. The shoe should bend—but in the right places. The flexibility should be fairly minimal at the back of the shoe, in the heel area, and pretty loose at the front of the shoe. When you run, your foot rolls in the front one-third of its length. That's where the shoe needs a smooth, easy bend. If it lacks it, then your leg will suffer from extra stress.

Once inside the shoe, your big toe should settle in about three-quarters of an inch short of the front of the shoe. On the sides, your feet should feel firmly enclosed but not too snug. It's a matter of degree, very personal, and only you can judge. If your foot width is a C or D—make sure, by the way, that you have your width checked by the shoe clerk and his measuring instrument — then you'll have no trouble finding the correct shoe. But there aren't too many brands of running shoes that accommodate customers outside those standard sizes. In a pinch, a fellow with a size B can use an insole to reduce the width of a shoe, but there's always a danger that an insole, incorrectly inserted, can cause problems for other parts of the foot. The safest bet if you own a foot that's hopelessly out of step is to invest money in hiring a shoemaker to custom make your shoes.

The final test for fit comes with action. Be brave. Take a short jog around the aisles and counters of the store.

Tops : The tops should mould fairly snugly over your toes and instep, not enough to cramp your running motion but hardly so loose that your skin suffers irritation. The tops of the toes are especially vulnerable to seams and lines in the shoe that scrape and chafe. If you suspect such grief during the fitting, you've got the wrong shoe. As for the exterior, nylon has the advantage in weight (it's light) and texture (it's soft), but in the long run, leather may be the winner for durability and sturdiness.

Arch : This is tricky because the arch's conformation differs perceptibly from foot to foot, jogger to jogger. Many shoes come with a built-in arch support, but the chances are that the support will be slightly out-of-whack for your foot. You should pay particular attention to the arch fit of the shoes you buy. If you need special support for your arch — a fact that will become clear to you after a few jogs — then a commercial product may handle your problem. Dr. Scholl's products offer a wide variety of arch supports. Some experienced runners build their own supports, "cookies" as they're known in the trade, out of surgical felt or foam rubber and then bind them into the shoe with adhesive tape. In any event, if you find yourself stuck with a shoe that has an incorrect arch, rip it out and replace it with a Dr. Scholl's support or with a homemade cookie (if you're a handy craftsman) or with a custom-moulded insert made for you by a podiatrist or shoemaker.

Socks: the Inside Story

Always wear white socks. If you put on blue socks, you're apt to find blue dye in the cracks of your feet. The same goes for red, green, purple, puce and all other colors in or out of the rainbow.

A few joggers can avoid the temptation of color by not wearing any socks. They run with skin next to shoe. But they're in a tiny minority. Most joggers require socks for a single reason: to prevent blisters. Many experienced distance runners find the best results with two pairs of socks, a thin cotton pair on the inside and a thicker pair on the outside. Try it. If it works for you, if you feel no blistering effects, stick with the dual protection. Otherwise, try a pair of singles. But watch out that you don't fill the inside of your shoe with socks that are too bulky. They'll cramp your feet and your style.

If, in spite of every precaution, you come down with a case of blisters, act pronto. Wash the foot. Apply an antiseptic to the blister and surrounding area. Cover with gauze. Tape in place. Sometimes you can head off blisters at the pass. When you detect a slight friction, even a simple tickle, in some part of your foot, don't ignore it. Lather Vaseline over the spot before you step out for your jog.

Speaking of feet ailments, some joggers fall victim to athlete's foot, the annoying fungus that usually gathers between the toes. If you notice signs of athlete's foot, wash the affected area thoroughly. Dab on a hygienic cleansing solution. And between treatments, sprinkle on talcum powder. Many joggers use talc as a matter of routine. It offers a pleasant sensation to the feet and helps keep them sweet and clean. If the hygienic solution doesn't cure your athlete's foot, then you've likely caught a more ferocious brand of fungus infection, and you should consult a doctor.

Shorts and Shirts and Stuff Underneath

There's only one hard and fast rule: wear clothes that are loose and comfortable. For many men, that rules out jockstraps. They rub the wrong way. Cotton jockey shorts will do the same job without chafing, though, for reasons that probably don't bear examination, many male American joggers report comfy success wearing women's nylon panties.

For men who are proud of their legs or who don't give a damn, a pair of running shorts and a T-shirt round out the clothing requirements. For all others, a warm-up suit covers a multitude of sins. Avoid a pure nylon suit. It doesn't absorb sweat as efficiently as a suit made of a cotton-nylon combination. Always choose clothes that absorb sweat but that are also loose enough to let out your body heat. Jeans are disqualified on the latter grounds, but an old pair of summer pants probably fills the bill as neatly as any gear from a sporting goods store. The important point, especially for beginners, is to jog in whatever clothes soothe and buoy your spirits as well as body. After all, when you're launching yourself on a brave new enterprise, you need all the psychological support you can muster.

Helpful hint: If any piece of clothing consistently irritates your skin, spread on Vaseline before your jog. Continue the practice until the irritation stops.

Obvious tip: Don't forget to put your jogging clothes through regular washes.

Final addendum for those who jog in extreme cold or heat: You'll need the extra clothing and other equipment that are listed in chapter five.

Spare Parts and Optional Extras

Luminous strips: If your jogging hours are after the sun has set — or before it's risen — stick luminous strips on your shoes and shirt. With such protection, you'll cut down on the number of cars that might sideswipe you on dark streets.

A handful of change: That's money. A quarter. A few dimes. Anything that'll make a pay phone function. You may need the coins in a scenario that goes like this: you're on a lengthy jog that takes you a mile or so from home base, and at the half-way mark, the sky that was cloudless when you began suddenly erupts, unleashing a storm of rain, wind and other hazards. Impossible to jog on without risk of chill and fever and tumbles on the wet pavement. What to do? Nonchalantly you step into a nearby drugstore, drop the coins carefully packed in your jogging attire into the pay phone and summon a lift from a willing chauffeur back home, or from the closest taxi stand.

Notebook: Keep a jogging diary. It serves a couple of useful purposes. The simple act of recording your yardage or mileage, with accompanying entries that note the weather, the state of your health and the nature of your adventures on the jog, helps foster the jogging habit. It's a fact of human nature that if you write about an activity, you give it fresh reality and permanence. The diary also serves as documentation of your program. Certainly at the beginning, it's best to put yourself on a jogging program that prescribes distances and times — see chapter three for program details — and a diary is the logical vehicle for keeping track of your progress. If you don't care for a diary, then make a large chart, something that shows all the days of the week for all the weeks of the year. Then in a space allotted for each detail, mark your time and distance under the appropriate day. Go ahead. Do it. It'll make you feel young and eager and efficient.

Stopwatch : Some exercise experts say a stopwatch, just its mere presence, makes a jogger too competitive for his own good. It challenges him and forces him to move beyond the level that suits his rate of progress. Wise advice perhaps, and a necessary note of caution, but not the final word on stopwatches. Beginning joggers will find a stopwatch helpful in two ways. One: to read the pulse rate. As chapter three will demonstrate, it's important to keep a check on your pulse, and a stopwatch is the best tool. Two: to time workouts. If you start on a program that calls for you to jog a couple of hundred yards in one minute and 55 seconds followed by 30 seconds of walking time, then, once again, a stopwatch eases the task. The idea isn't to jog against the clock. The idea is to jog with the clock. Eliminate competition. Make friends with your stopwatch. Make friends with all your equipment.

Dos and Don'ts

*Don't let cramped feet cramp your style
*Choose clothes that absorb sweat.
*Make friends with your equipment.
*Jog with the clock — not against it.

3

The Jogger's First Step

Getting started.
That's the toughest step
in a jogger's career.
It calls for a doctor's
okay, a fitness test,
a program of action, a
mastering of running style
—and plenty of determination.

Here's a quote: "Do *not* keep track of how far you go. Just keep moving for 20 to 30 minutes. As the weeks pass, you'll find yourself traveling farther without added effort. Vary the pace. Take interesting routes. If you wish, increase the time for each session. Enjoy yourself."

Now, with that admonition in mind, how do you launch yourself on a jogging program? The short answer is expressed in two words. Start slowly. The long answer is more complex, and it begins with a series of tests.

Playing It Safe

Some ailments and diseases make jogging—hard luck—out of the question for their victims. Serious diabetes is one, then some kidney and liver troubles, advanced arthritis, consistent pain in the lower part of the back. There are others, some of them slightly exotic, some revealed only on a doctor's examination. A thorough medical checkup is the essential first step to embarking on your jogging career. Tell the doctor what your plans are. Ask if he can find any reason for not following through on the plans. This procedure is called Playing It Safe.

Heart troubles don't necessarily rule out a jogging program. Dr. Terence Kavanagh is witness to that truth. He is the Medical Director of the Toronto Rehabilitation Centre, and in a pioneering program carried out through the 1970s, he has taken heart-attack victims and restored them to apparently sound health through a prescription of regular jogging and running. Studies of his patients reveal that they have recorded a non-fatal recurrence of heart attacks of 1.5 percent and of fatal recurrence of 1.4 percent as against non-fatal recurrence in the general population of seven to 13 percent and fatal recurrence of six to 12 percent. A remarkable achievement — perhaps even more remarkable is that some of Kavanagh's patients have finished the Boston Marathon—but the fact still remains that heart ailments, actual or incipient, may make jogging out of the question for those unfortunate men and women who suffer from them. Therefore an electrocardiogram is a necessity in any pre-jogging checkup. But it must be noted that EKGs taken at rest do not always reveal every possible problem. "To be of real value," writes Dr. Gabe Mirkin, an American physician who takes a special interest in runners, "an EKG must be done during exertion. A 'stress' cardiogram may pick up left ventricle strain or a poor blood supply to the heart." The stress cardiogram is usually carried out by having the patient pedal a stationary bicycle or run on a treadmill while he's hooked up to machines tracing his heart's reactions. Very few doctors are equipped with such facilities, but the beginning jogger is advised to seek a physician who can accommodate a stress cardiogram. That's playing it safe.

Testing for Fitness

Want some more tests? There are more, the kind that indicate exactly (or as exactly as possible) how far or how long you ought to jog at the beginning of your program. You can administer them yourself or consult one of the fitness institutes or health clubs that have sprung up in the 1970s. Many of these enterprising organizations are equipped to test for strength, flexibility, heart reserve, maximum oxygen uptake and all the other measuring sticks of fitness. Many are in a position to administer stress cardiograms, but all too often the club attendants handling the tests aren't qualified to read them for indications of lurking heart problems. A curious conundrum: doctors lack the equipment for stress cardiograms but possess the expertise, health clubs own the machines but not the know-how. Still, the clubs and institutes offer rewarding guidance in calculating your fitness and in directing you to a jogging schedule that suits the calculations. All you need is the time and money to take them up on the offer.

As for the self-administered fitness tests, there are basically two.

The Cooper Test. How much ground can you get over in 12 minutes? Try it over a quarter-mile track or some other pre-measured area. Walk, run, jog, crawl. Keep moving for 12 minutes. Then measure the distance of your walking, running, jogging and crawling *in toto*. Take the figure and apply it against Dr. Cooper's charts, which employ a built-in formula to indicate your maximum oxygen uptake and, from that statistic, your level of fitness. If you cover less than a mile in 12 minutes, then, according to the charts, your Cooper fitness category is Very Poor. Other distances indicate, on the Cooper scale, categories of Poor, Fair, Good and Excellent, and for each category, Dr. Cooper prescribes a fixed set of exercise programs to suit the indicated state of fitness. For those beginning joggers who respond to a challenging, scientific, goal-oriented and slightly rigid program, then Dr. Cooper's system, outlined in his book *Aerobics*, is just the ticket. Even for those who don't care to lock themselves into such a program, the 12-minute test is still useful. If you cover a mile and a quarter, you're in poor shape, at least by Dr. Cooper's standards. Up to a mile and a half, you're fair; above that and up to a mile and three-quarters makes you in good shape; and anything over 1.75 miles qualifies you as excellent for fitness.

The Balke Test. This test, plotted by an authority in exercise physiology named Dr. Bruno Balke, calls for 15 minutes of moving on foot. You must take the measurement of the distance you cover in that time in meters. One mile equals 1609.354 meters. Divide the figure you arrive at — distance in meters — by 15. That gives you a number for your speed in meters per minute. Now apply a formula: (your speed minus 133) times .172 plus 33.3. The figure you end up with after that arithmetical maneuver is your maximum oxygen uptake. To find out where your score places you in the fitness scale, check the chart at the end of this chapter.

There are two fine points raised by these self-administered tests.

1. They're strenuous. Indeed, if you're overweight and under-exercised, they might be impossible and too risky to attempt. Dr. Cooper recognizes the danger. "If you are over 35," he writes, "and have not been exercising regularly, do not take the initial 12-minute test." Instead, he advises, you should proceed directly to a program that gets you started by walking one mile per day. The physical difficulty in testing out-of-condition subjects also applies to procedures in fitness clubs — some people simply do not possess the leg strength to pedal a stationary bicycle long enough to record a reading. If you belong to that category, don't panic. Forget the testing, and get yourself launched on an exercise schedule that begins with relatively easy walks.

2. Maybe the best test of all is a consultation with your own body. How fit does it feel? Can it manage a good stiff mile-long walk? Would a jog down the block wipe it out? Take a walk or jog — nothing torturous — and discuss the result with your body. It knows best how it reacts. Let it tell you how much stress it can safely take. Then make a rational decision about the type of program to follow.

The Pep Talk

You've been cleared by your doctor, you've measured yourself on the tests you're able to take, and you're almost ready to slide out the front door in your new jogging gear. But, first, allow time for some mental stock-taking. Admit to yourself that you rank low on the fitness scale. Consider the struggle ahead. Does it look uphill? Groan — it probably does.

Now read the words of Joe Henderson, a runner and the editor of *Runner's World* magazine. Early in 1976, on the occasion of National Running Week in the United States, he addressed some advice to beginning joggers that was designed to prepare them for the rigors and disappointments, trials and tribulations to come.

"If you're going to be honest with yourself," Henderson said, "then I should be equally honest by telling you that the first weeks, maybe even months, of running will be no fun. It will be tiring. It will hurt. Even the slowest shuffle will be difficult because you're asking your body to do something it hasn't done in a long time — if ever. You will dread it because no sane person looks forward to pain. It will bore you because you aren't yet experiencing anything except fatigue, and boredom and fatigue are close relatives."

Whew! But — don't give up before you start — Henderson also offered some encouragement.

"All I can do," he said, "is ask you to bear up. Be strong and patient. Promise yourself you'll stick out this break-in period, and I promise you much better days to come."

Those better days arrive only for joggers who make their jogging into a habit, who make their jogs and runs fit into their lives with regularity. And that, once you've rallied from Joe Henderson's strong language, is the key. Make jogging a habit. Make it into what experienced runners and joggers proudly describe as "a positive addiction."

The Warm-up

Hold on. Don't step out the door. Not quite yet. It's best not to go into a jog with a cold body. Give it a warm-up. The process for beginning joggers should be gentle. Then, as the jogs grow in time and length, as the habit takes hold, the warm-up period will become more varied and complex.

For starters, do a little stretching. Roll your neck four or five times in small circles. That's to loosen the bunched-up muscles near the upper spine. Hunch and roll your shoulders, moving them back and forth three or four times to loosen chest and back muscles. Stick out your stomach, roll your hips, pull in your gut. Nothing too rambunctious. Just loosen your body. Place one foot out behind you, toe on the floor, heel raised, and rotate it clockwise five or six times. Now counterclockwise. Repeat procedure with the other foot. Simple exercises, but they get the juices flowing and the circulatory-muscular system activated.

As time and jogs go by, warm-up routines can grow more ambitious and, in fact, become an integral part of an overall fitness program. They might include sets of five to 15 sit-ups with 25-second rest periods between each set; four or five pushups repeated three times with rests between each; semi-splits (place left foot about a yard behind right foot, both aiming in the same direction and with hands on hips, slowly lower body towards floor, dropping the left leg, bending the right; do it five times and repeat with legs switched); high leg stretches (place one leg on a table or other piece of furniture that is about waist high, then with hands on the outstretched leg, lower your head as close to the leg as possible; repeat five times, then switch legs). There are other warm-up exercises, all calculated to loosen and strengthen muscles and tendons that come into play during a jog or run. They're helpful—and fun, too—but the essential point is not to rush into them. Add exercises to your jogging routine as your body is able to accommodate them. Otherwise, you may pull a muscle, strain a tendon or inflict a more serious injury on your unprepared body.

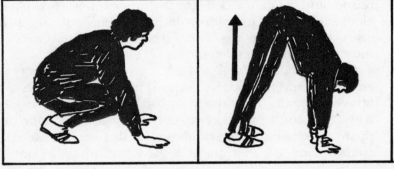

Recommended warm-up exercises for joggers

Jogging in Style

An English gentlewoman of the nineteenth century named Mrs. Edmund Caster sat at her desk one day and penned a few lines that could have been aimed at jogging folk of the twentieth century:

"The Centipede was happy quite,
Until the Toad in fun
Said 'Pray which leg goes after which?'
And worked her mind to such a pitch,
She lay distracted in the ditch
Considering how to run."

Moral for joggers: don't get so wrapped up in technique that you forget how to move. That said, it must also be pointed out that there are rights and wrongs about the style of jogging, ways of carrying your body, placing your feet and swinging your arms that make the jog more rewarding and other ways that turn it into an exhausting nightmare. Here are some basic guidelines to a good jogging style.

Body. Your center of gravity should always be over the front foot, the one that's just about to land. That calls for a slight forward lean of the body. Very slight. Keep your trunk reasonably erect. Relax your shoulders. Many joggers tend to bunch up their shoulders, stiffen their necks, and they often complain of an annoying tight feeling in that area after each jog. Hold your head in its normal position, not staring fixedly at the track or ground in front of you.

Feet. Don't land on your toes. That's for guys who are contending for a world record in the 100-meter dash. On the other hand, don't pound your heel into the track or ground. That's for guys who are going to end up with heel bruises or even worse troubles. There are, generally speaking, two correct ways to land. Bill Gairdner, a former Olympic athlete, describes one method: "The heel should strike the ground very softly. Roll through onto the ball of the foot and push off on the next stride." The other method, a very subtle variation, is recommended by trainers and other running advisers for middle-aged or beginning joggers, and it consists simply of landing flat-footed. Nothing forced, nothing pounding, just a relaxed flat-footed style, which comes naturally when the jogger uses a proper short stride.

Stride. Keep it short. Depending on your height, that means a stride of not more than four feet and probably more in the two-to-three foot range. Be economical. Long striding wastes energy and contributes to injury.

Arms. They act as a balance mechanism, the right arm balancing the left leg, the left arm taking care of the right leg. Incorrect arm movement can throw you out of kilter. It can also make you jog faster than you might care to; that happens when you swing your arms too quickly, an action that translates into a pick-up of speed in the legs. So, don't carry your arms too high (pumping above the shoulders), don't carry them too low (dropping below the hips) and don't swing them across your body (leading to a side-to-side motion). The best bet is to bend the arms at something close to a 90-degree angle, and swing them back and forth above the hips, reaching just slightly in front of the body.

Hitting your Stride

"Don't go out and jog a mile," says Paul Lessack, chief exercise physiologist at Rutgers University in New Jersey. "Jog for a minute and walk for a minute. Repeat that five or six times."

"I train everyone, even world-record holders, the same way," says Dr. Ernst van Aaken, the respected German track coach and physiologist. "I have them mix together comfortable runs with breaks for walking."

The Bowerman and Harris program for men and women who are in average condition: "Day one. Jog 55 yards. Walk 55 yards. Repeat four times. Jog 110 yards. Walk 110 yards. Repeat four times. Jog 55 yards. Walk 55 yards. Repeat four times."

See the consistency in these views and systems? All reflect one aspect of what Bowerman calls "the hard-easy principle." For beginners, there's no need, according to this notion, to attempt a consecutive one-mile jog. Alternate jogging and walking. Jog from one lamppost to the next, walk from it to the

Recommended jogging postures

Hold your head normally. Your neck should not be tense

The correct jogging stride

**Proper
arm position**

Recommended foot landing position

third, jog to the fourth and so on around the block. The jog starts you on the long road to fitness, and the walk provides you with a balancing breather.

Eventually, as your days of jogging stretch into the future and as your strength increases, you'll probably find yourself eager and capable of jogging longer distances with fewer walking intervals or with no walking intervals. Maybe you'll jog five or six miles. Maybe you'll become addicted to LSD, which, in Dr. Terence Kavanagh's lexicon, stands for "long slow distance." So much the better. But for starters — and maybe forever — apply the hard-easy principle. Alternate walks and jogs. It's a method with a proven record of success.

That gets you off the mark. It also leaves some unanswered questions.

1. *What if your physical condition, at the beginning of your jogging program, doesn't permit you to jog, even in alternation with walks?* Then forget jogging and walk. That's all. Walk. Try walking for ten or 15 minutes. It's a start — and the essential rule in the whole enterprise is that whatever you are, walker, jogger or runner, you must establish the starting pace suitable to your own individual capabilities. Let the eager beaver next door rip off his eight-minute miles. If your body—with a word or two from your doctor—tells you that a ten-minute walk is your starting point, then settle for the gentle pace. Try it four or five times a week until your body signs indicate you can hang in for longer periods. Work up to a 30-minute daily walk. Maybe you'll never progress beyond that point. Okay, settle for it. But the chances are that the walks will condition you for something speedier.

2. *How fast should you jog?* Bowerman suggests the talk test. If you can carry on a chat as you move, then you've arrived at a good pace. If you have trouble gasping out the words, then you're moving too quickly for your own good. Suppose there's nobody to talk to? Then try singing a tune to yourself and apply the same principle. If you can't project the lyrics without wheezing for air, then you're not absorbing a proper supply of oxygen. Slow down. When you take up the interval scheme — jog, walk, jog, walk, *ad infinitum* — you might try jogging until your breathing gets heavy. Then walk briskly as

far as it takes for you to recover. That procedure, as a means of testing your pace, applies only after you've broken your body into a regular jogging program.

3. *How do you recognize progress?* At the beginning, in the first few weeks, progress is the key. If you don't feel that you're progressing, then you may, in a pique of discouragement, chuck the whole idea of getting fit through jogging. What complicates the situation is that progress is personal. Only *you* can judge if *you* are moving ahead. In order to gain improvement in fitness, you must place some stress on your system. You must overload your body to a certain degree. In doing this there are two rules to follow: try harder and be honest. Try harder to extend the distance and times of your jogs and be honest in judging how much effort you're investing. Don't dog it. Naturally you must practice caution, especially at the beginning of the program, but once you're well launched, you've got to challenge yourself. *Then* you'll experience progress. Perhaps the most convenient measuring stick is a stopwatch, or at least a watch with a second hand that's easy to read. You can bring it into play in two ways. Using the watch as a guide, jog for straight periods of time, increasing the period each week. Three straight minutes in week five, four in week six and so on. That's employing the watch in a way that makes time the measuring factor. Or, following Bowerman's system, you can use the watch to set a pace for distance. In the Bowerman scheme, for example, a man or woman in average condition progresses from jogging at a rate of 55 to 60 seconds for every 110-yard distance in the first week to jogging at a rate of 25 to 30 seconds for 110 yards in the twelfth week. *That's* progress.

4. *How do you shape a regular program?* Keep a notebook. Mark down distances and times. Add passing remarks on your condition. Note improvements. The jottings, you'll find, bring continuity to your jogging program. Subscribing to an established program such as the Cooper system or the Bowerman plan will help you structure your jogging. Or, relying on your instincts and your body's messages, you may fashion a personal program. Set small objectives for yourself measured in terms of time or of distance. If you feel comfortable walking and jogging around the block at the end of week one, then try

walking and jogging around the block one and a half times in week two. Trust your body signs. Jot the distances in your notebook. If all signals seem to be for two blocks in week three, then move up. That's continuity. That's regularity. Your program will gradually take shape. Or you might base your efforts on increased time, launching yourself with ten daily minutes of walking-jogging in week one and gradually increasing the dosage by five-minute chunks. Before you realize what wonders you have wrought, you'll have the jogging habit.

5. *How much time should you set aside for each day's jog?* Let's assume that you're in average condition or you're past the stage where your legs can manage no more than a 15-minute walk. Then the answer to the question is this: ideally, 45 minutes to one hour. That's in total. That includes time to put on your jogging duds, loosen up, hit the road or track, unwind, shower and change. By permitting yourself a full hour, you're able to seal yourself off from the distractions that might make you rush through your workout and leave you with the nagging doubt that you haven't reaped all its benefits. Joe Henderson, the editor of *Runner's World* magazine, has best described the state of mind you should look for during your jogging period. "Make your hour a sacred one. Give half of it to activity, half to inactivity, and don't hurry through either one. Get away from the props and demands of civilization — the car, TV, newspapers, job — and be primitive for awhile. Make this your most creative time."

6. *How much of the hour should be invested in action?* At least 30 minutes. Better if it's 40. That's time for jogging, running, walking or moving any way you can invent. The first five to ten minutes of any jog are inevitably given over to working out the kinks, making the juices flow and kicking over the body's engine. During this period, you're not offering your body much conditioning impact. If you stopped after ten minutes, you wouldn't have advanced your fitness by much more than a single beat. It's the 15 or 20 minutes that follow the initial period that yield the dividends. By then, your body has activated what track people call "the training effect." The heart pumps, the blood flows — and you're getting fit.

7. *How many days of the week should you jog?* "Most effec-

tive of all," Lloyd Percival, for years the leading Canadian fitness spokesman, once said, "is two days' work followed by a day of rest. Recovery is part of training. Least effective is exercise two days a week or less." What Percival suggests is another aspect of the work-rest principle, and most exercise physiologists agree with him that a regimen that alternates days of jogging and days of rest produces excellent fitness results. In short, there's no need for you to hit the jogging path seven days a week in religious devotion. Even God took a rest on the seventh day. But, at the same time, you must bear in mind the wisdom behind Dr. Terence Kavanagh's pep talk to his patients: "You can't build up a state of exercise or fitness that can be used over later months or years of sedentary living." For satisfying results, you should adjust your schedule for four and preferably five days of jogging per week. Not every day needs to include the same jog. Nor does every day of rest need to be entirely idle. As you develop a measure of fitness — and of confidence — you can follow a varied pattern, something like the following:

Day one: One hour of alternate jogs and walks.

Day two: An easy 30-minute walk through the neighborhood.

Day three: A good, hard, hour-long jog with fewer walks.

Day four: Rest. Short easy walk after dinner.

Day five: One hour of alternate jogs and walks.

Day six: Game of tennis singles.

Day seven: One hour of jogs and walks.

On the other hand, you might grow so hooked on jogging that you prefer a solid hour's jog five times a week. Or maybe you get into running. Maybe you've even caught the ambition to run the Boston Marathon. Wherever you end, the place to start is with four or five days per week of jogs and walks and runs.

Time of Day — or Night

Dr. Kenneth Cooper runs at five o'clock in the afternoon. "My work is done," he writes, "and the running works off any tensions that may have accumulated." Many businessmen all over the world rush from their offices to a nearby track, indoor or outdoor, at noon. It fits neatly into the day's schedule, and after they've developed a consistent noon-hour jogging routine, they find they have plenty of energy and not much need for a heavy lunch. And then there's the English jogger who wrote about his schedule in this way: "I try to do my three miles at six in the morning. That means I've got the thing done, and for the rest of the day, I can work, eat, drink and chase girls. It's like the confessional. Once it's over with, you're released."

Take your pick. The time of day when you do your jog is tied up with the nature of your job, the demands of your family, your psychology and a half-dozen other physical, mental and spiritual factors. Time is a variable, but from the experience of most joggers, it's at least true that, once you arrive at the most suitable time of day for yourself, you get the best results by sticking, day in and day out, to that time period. Joggers who jog at six a.m. on day one, noon on day two and midnight on day three are most often joggers who eventually abandon their programs. A consistent jogging time is not an arbitrary rule, but one of the many aids a jogger uses to enforce his commitment to regular exercise.

That's one rule — jog at the same time of day for each workout — and here are two more modest rules.

1. Wait a sensible interval after a meal before you set foot on the track or street or path. In the period immediately following lunch or dinner or breakfast, your blood is busy in the stomach aiding the process of digestion. It isn't ready to flow into the legs to offer support during the jog. And there's another sound reason to wait out the digestion period: if you don't, you may find yourself feeling nauseated in mid-jog.

2. If evening is your most convenient jogging time, allow at least one hour after the jog before bedtime. Your body needs a minimum of 60 minutes to unwind before it will be relaxed enough to sleep.

The Warm-down

It begins while you're still on the jogging trail or track, and it's a

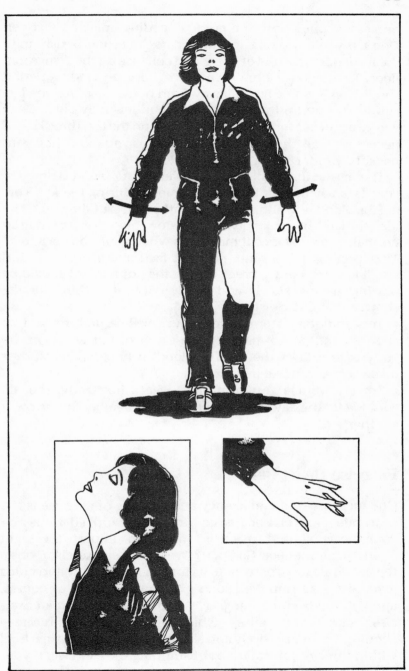

Recommended warm-down exercises

process of tailing off in a gradual, gliding, relaxing manner. Don't, if you're jogging around the neighborhood, rush up to the front door in a trail of sweat and collapse on the livingroom floor. That's no time to warm down. Your unwinding period should begin a few blocks away from home base. Jog the last couple of hundred yards at a slow and leisurely pace. Or, if you're on an indoor track, take it slowly on the last three laps. If necessary, walk them. Shake your arms as you move. Roll your neck. Unwind. Loosen up. Warm down.

The reason for all this care is because your blood is down in your legs where your body dispatched it during the jog. That means blood is in short supply in other parts of the body. The idea, in fact the necessity, is to restore blood distribution to normal, to the balance it maintains when your body is at rest. That process takes time, perhaps five or ten minutes, and you'll give the body a break during the adjustment period by moving around slowly and gently without rushing for the shower, car, chair or bed.

Ten minutes later comes your well-earned reward: a shower. Not too hot because the effect of hot water on the body is to reduce the flow of blood in circulation. Make it lukewarm and make it relaxed.

Towel off. Smile. You're entitled to feel a little smug. After all, your jog for the day is behind you. But, remember tomorrow is another jog.

Exercise Heart Rate

One measure of the efficiency and benefits of exercise is the heart rate. "Exercise heart rate" is the term applied to the rate your heart should reach in order to impart the right strengthening effect. Got that? Well, proper exercise boosts the heart rate to 70 percent of its maximum capacity and holds it there for 12 minutes. Such exertion does not, of course, apply to the beginning jogger. When you're starting an exercise program, your pulse —which indicates your heart rate— shouldn't rise excessively and should return to its normal level within three or four minutes of stopping the exercise. If your

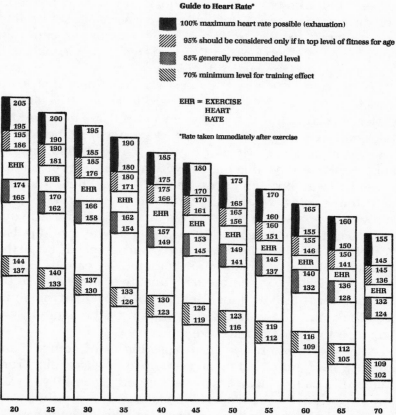

Guide to Heart Rate*

■ 100% maximum heart rate possible (exhaustion)

▨ 95% should be considered only if in top level of fitness for age

▤ 85% generally recommended level

▧ 70% minimum level for training effect

EHR = EXERCISE
HEART
RATE

*Rate taken immediately after exercise

Exercise cardiologists and other jogging experts have slightly varying opinions on the exact levels for the Exercise Heart Rate. The chart shown here generally indicates levels to guide joggers who have at least a few months' experience at regular jogging.

Warning: The use of the Guide to Heart Rate assumes no underlying heart or respiratory disease, or other condition which could be adversely affected by exercise. A medical consultation is recommended before starting an exercise program.

pulse is pounding too fast, then cool it. You're pushing yourself too hard too soon. But if you are a jogger nicely settled into your program, a consistent boost in the heart rate means that you're doing the job for your heart, strengthening it, making it work under a high oxygen demand.

To measure your exercise heart rate you must first learn how to read your pulse. Use the carotid artery. It is slightly easier to read than the traditional wrist pulse. The carotid is the large artery in the front of the neck located on either side of the Adam's apple. Place your hand in the immediate vicinity and you'll find it beating merrily with a good vigorous pump.

Got it? Okay, but don't press too hard. That could interfere with the reading. Now that you feel it pumping, take your stopwatch or a watch with a large second indicator in your other hand and start counting the beats of the carotid pulse. You're going to count for ten seconds. And when you begin the count, you begin by saying zero. As the pulse beats and as the seconds click by, you count zero, one, two, three and so on until ten seconds have gone fleeing by. At the end of that time, take the count you've reached and multiply the figure by six. Presto — that's your heart rate.

What you're interested in discovering is, of course, your *exercise* heart rate. That means you must take a reading from the carotid pulse as soon as you've stopped jogging. If you wait any longer, anything beyond ten seconds after stopping, your heart will be returning to its normal rate. Checking the carotid within the ten-second limit will present you with an accurate enough indication of your exercise heart rate. And with that information, you'll be in a position to judge the nature of your jog. Too fast? Too slow? The exercise heart rate will let you know. But how do you recognize *your* particular exercise heart rate? And, more important, how do you calculate it? That's the second lesson. Fortunately there are a couple of handy-dandy formulas. Most exercise physiologists recognize two sorts of exercise heart rate: Minimum Exercise Heart Rate for those in average shape and Maximum Exercise Heart Rate for those who are growing more fit. Here's the generally accepted formula for each:

Minimum Exercise Heart Rate: 170 minus your age.

Maximum Exercise Heart Rate: 200 minus your age.

Thus, if you happen to be 44, your minimum exercise heart rate would be 126 and your maximum 156, which suggests that if you are age 44 and in not-so-sensational condition, you shouldn't let your heart race any higher than 126 during exercise but that you can push for 156 as you become better conditioned. Some coaches indicate that the maximum could rise slightly higher, up to 160 for a 44-year-old for example, but the easily remembered formula shown above is probably as convenient and trustworthy a guide as any.

Dos and Don'ts

*Get the jogging habit.
*Practice the hard-easy principle.
*Take time to warm up and warm down.
*Make your jogging hour into a sacred period.

Grass, Cement and Boards

What's the best surface for jogging?
The most congenial landscape?
The experienced jogger learns to adapt his
jogging to the advantages and drawbacks
of all types of environment and to welcome the
variety they bring to his program.

$\mathbf{M}$eet Tom Alderman, a pioneer jogger who earns his living as a peripatetic journalist. Tom started jogging in 1965, long before such an outrageous activity had occurred to most citizens. "It was the year when my waist size went from 30 to 33," he says. "That was an intimation of my mortality." He took to jogging, beginning by covering one mile on each of three mornings per week. Today, his daily average is four or five miles of running six mornings a week. "I've got legs like Johnny Bench's," Tom says, "and I'm ready to roar all day."

That's Tom the happy jogger. Now let's move along to Tom the peripatetic journalist. He works out of Toronto, but "out of" is the operative phrase. Tom flies all over the world tracking down stories. He puts in a few days in New York, a weekend in Newfoundland, a fast hop to a European capital. And wherever he travels, he takes along his jogging self. Tom has run in all sorts of geography, on all types of physical surface and under every conceivable circumstance. Here he is, by way of illustration, offering a condensed version of his jogging experiences in a few of the centers that his globe-trotting profession has taken him to:

Vancouver: "They've got Stanley Park, nothing but trees and grass and water close to the center of the city. Peaceful, easy, contemplative. I once jogged past Muhammad Ali in Stanley Park. He was training for a title fight in Vancouver. He won. I attribute his victory to the beauty of Stanley Park."

Martinique: "Dirt roads. They give you trouble because of pot holes and other hazards. The local people are very poor and they think you're crazy to do anything that isn't work and isn't rest. To them, a jogger is the week's best laugh."

New York City: "I once jogged through Central Park at seven in the morning with six New Yorkers who are regular runners. They figure there's strength in numbers and besides, they move too quickly for muggers. It was one of the fastest jogs I ever had, but the paths were very nice for scenery and for foot comfort."

Montreal: "Whenever I go there, I take the same route, along Sherbrooke Street, up Côte des Neiges and around Mount Royal Park. That's a classy section of town, which is what a jogger should look for in big cities. In Philadelphia, I jogged around Rittenhouse Square. Very ritzy. In Boston, it was up the Charles River and back. Same thing. Joggers need a little ritz in their lives."

And so on.

The lesson that a jogger may take from Tom Alderman is straightforward: there are pleasures to be found in almost every geographical location, every physical surface, every landscape and cityscape. A jogger can do his number anywhere. The only catch is that some spots and some underfoot conditions demand adjustment. Maybe a change in equipment is needed or, more likely, a change in attitude or approach. Some surfaces, no doubt, are more suited to jogging than others. So are some sections of a country or a continent. City running? *Inner* city running? Country running? Valleys? Mountains? Highways? You can try them all if you adapt to their differences.

The Pleasures and Pitfalls of Grass

Many jogging gurus champion grass as the most agreeable surface. Grass contains a built-in spring that offers comfort to the foot. The principal areas of pain for joggers, especially beginners, are the ankles, knees and other joints, and grass provides the best cushion against such aches. Grass is also effective as a psychological boost. When a jogger bounces gently across the greensward, he takes on the confidence and panache of a genuine and dedicated long-distance runner, and the resulting mental boost often works to jack up his morale. He can jog longer and further and still feel buoyant.

But, be warned, grass is deceptive. Too often, under the green smoothness, there are bumps and ruts, miniature valleys and hillocks of earth. An uneven surface can disrupt your stride, throw you off balance and strain ligaments and tendons that, likely as not, are already putting up with as much stress as they care to bear.

The danger of the uneven turf is increased when it's grown hard and tough under a baking sun. A case in point may be found in an examination of the 1974 American Athletic Union marathon championship. Most marathons in the US are held on parkland, over turf that's resilient, but in 1974, the locale was Belmont, California, across earth packed so hard that it turned the run into a cruel grind. Within a couple of miles of the beginning of the race, many competitors had tumbled off their feet, suffering from gruesomely twisted ankles. Their agony didn't stem so much from the hardness of the ground as from the *combination* of unresisting clay and bumpy surface. Any jogger can compensate for a hard surface with proper shoes, but when the ground is also deceptively uneven, then sprains and falls lie ahead for the unwary.

City people should search out the best grass expanses in parks and ravines, adjacent to reservoirs and around the borders of cemeteries; but remember always to check that nature hasn't booby-trapped the dulcet green.

Highways and Byways

There are several advantages to jogging on paved surfaces.

1. A road lies as close as your front door, thereby eliminating time-consuming drives to a track or park.

2. Cement is relatively smooth, and any pitfalls and traps are easily spotted.

3. Proper equipment and proper running style will overcome cement's physical shortcomings. Wear sturdy shoes with thick solid soles. And don't land on the surface as if you intend to drive your foot through the cement. Sure, you may experience some mild aches and pains, especially if you've just launched your jogging career, but in 99 percent of cases, the discomfort will be minor. If you develop shin splints, tenderness in the front or side of the shin bone, then you can always switch temporarily to a softer running surface.

Warning: Automobiles are a jogger's natural foe. The odds, however, are all on the auto's side, and in a contest between a 2,000-pound car and a 150-pound jogger, it's a fond farewell to the jogger. All of which makes plain sense, but the crazy truth is that many joggers, moving in breezy triumph down a highway or a dark street, develop a streak of testy arrogance and refuse to budge for an oncoming or following car. When it comes to automobiles, the rule for the fellow on foot is to practice defensive running. Watch for cars and give them a wide berth. They may not be watching or moving for you.

Indoor Tracks

Boredom is the chief drawback to indoor running. Most indoor tracks, particularly those built in such profusion in recent years as adjuncts to gymnasiums, health clubs and squash clubs, demand as many as 24 circuits to make up a mile. Thus, a one-mile jog means 24 laps around the same unvarying scenery, and it means 96 repetitive corners in the eight or more minutes it takes to finish the course. A steady diet of such jogs tends to numb the mind and ultimately discourage the jogger. Still, it's easy enough to trick the brain into thinking it's enjoying itself. Play games with your jog. Test yourself for a few laps by dogging the heels of a runner who's slightly more swift than you. Practice running high on the banked boards as you approach a curve, then cutting low across the curve in an accelerated zoom. A little childish maybe, but it can be entertaining and make you feel like Paavo Nurmi or Roger Bannister.

As well as playing games, observe some track tips:

1. If you use a track frequently, four or more times a week, change the direction in which you run on alternate days. Run counter-clockwise on Mondays, clockwise on Tuesdays, counter-clockwise on Wednesdays, and so on. The purpose behind alternating is to avoid the orthopedic problems that can crop up from constantly running on a surface that is sloped in one downward direction. What you must do is vary the slope. If the track gets plenty of business, speak to the gym or club director and persuade him to post signs that make it a track policy to switch the running direction for everyone on alternate days.

2. Carry a lap counter in your hand and punch up the number of circuits you're making as you complete them. It's maddening to keep count in your head and more maddening to forget your count. Many clubs have a supply of counters on hand. If not, most sporting goods stores will sell you one for five bucks.

3. Use the track as an indoor refuge in stormy weather or as a variation on outdoor jogging. The evidence is that too many joggers who confine themselves to tracks eventually abandon their jogging programs. It takes a determined mind to cope with the constant tedium of the track. Tracks are handy for downtown office workers and a godsend in the most bitter winter weather. But the best advice is not to rely exclusively on the indoor boards.

Downtown Jogging

"Look for the nice part of town," says Tom Alderman, the jogger-journalist. "That's the rule. You have to find something to occupy your mind or you'll go mad."

Well, the situation isn't quite *that* menacing, but there are rules that add pleasure and safety to the city jog.

1. Old residential areas are always surefire territory for jogging because in almost every city in the world, such areas offer pleasantly meandering streets, interesting architecture, tall trees and tolerant citizens. A dynamite combination.

2. Stay away from apartment building complexes. High winds tend to whistle dangerously around such areas, and they force the jogger to waste valuable energy in sustaining his pace.

3. Avoid routes that take you in the direction of traffic lights and pedestrian congestion. Otherwise your jog loses its momentum in a series of stops, bumps, stumbles and confused collisions.

4. Wherever you run, map out a course. Drive your car around the running neighborhood and calculate distances on the car's odometer. Arrange a one- or two-mile route with variations that add on more miles as desired. And be sure that the route is roughly circular, leading you back home or back to your car and not to the other side of town.

5. Watch out for curbstones.

Country Jogging

Ah, the zen of it all! The spirituality! The mind-blowing beauty! Or, as John Christian put it, Mr. Christian having the good fortune to jog each morning through his place of employment, a 2,000-acre park reserve a few miles outside of Minneapolis: "I am alone with myself but feel unity with the world around me. My personal problems of the day and world affairs shrink in a forest of trees, lakes and meadows, and the openness and awareness with the great earth. I feel a special closeness to the natural wonders and realize more clearly my niche in this

complex web of life." Purple prose perhaps, but still packed
with truth. Country jogging works wonders for the psyche. It
gives the jogger a sense of sniffing life's flowers and, in practi-
cal terms, it encourages him to cover more territory, without
straining, than he is likely to in less genial surroundings.

Let us pause for an instant, however, to consider a few
cautions:

1. For a city dweller, country jogging takes an investment in
time to drive to and from the country jogging site. A run
through forest and field must therefore become a sometime
thing and is probably most rewarding if it's set aside as a treat,
something to do on a Sunday as a special prize for all those
weekday mornings spent on pavement and boards.

2. Check out your country locale with care. You can, after all,
get yourself lost or run into an unfriendly farmer who doesn't
cotton to damn fool city folks actin' like fools. Dogs are
another potential threat. For some reason, country dogs go in
for more nipping at joggers' heels than city dogs do. The urban
canines have probably learned to accept joggers as a fact of a
dog's life. In any event, the rule is to scout your country route
in advance.

3. Don't get carried away. It's easy, lulled by rural beauty, to
run too far and too fast. Don't overextend your capabilities.
Don't jog, mind blank of all but the surrounding beauties, and
find yourself a half-dozen miles from your car, out of wind and
energy to walk back to it. Plan the logistics of your run along a
nice circular route that brings you back to the family sedan.

4. Don't jog it alone. Imagine the very worst. Imagine a
twisted ankle, a severe attack of shin splints, a pulled muscle.
And imagine yourself isolated in strange territory with no one
to hear your groans. Be wise. Pack along a friendly fellow
jogger.

5. Cool it on hills. Running in an upwards direction gobbles
up oxygen. The effect, if you push too hard, is like holding your
breath underwater. Lungs burst, legs turn to lead, the whole
body screams, especially muscles that don't come into play
during flat running but receive a severe testing on hills.

Jogging on Foreign Soil

The main obstacle that the jogger in a foreign country must overcome is his inhibition, as an American businessman and runner named Stephen Wald discovered when he visited Moscow in 1975. Not long after his flight landed, Mr. Wald felt the urge for a refreshing jog. But, he later wrote, "I had some concern. A matter as simple as an unaccompanied run through Moscow is an unusual activity—and unusual acitivity is not encouraged in the Soviet Union." Nevertheless, he plunged forth, and in no time at all, jogging smoothly, he was admiring the red star on top of the Kremlin and the peak of Ivan the Great's Bell Tower. He shed his inhibitions, jogged on, and apart from the exotic scenery, felt as much at home as he did back on the pavement of the good old USA.

At first blush, a visitor to a foreign city might come down with a fit of shy reluctance when it comes time for his daily jog. Stephen Wald's answer, and Tom Alderman's, too, comes in a single word: relax. "So some senorita may giggle at your hairy legs on the elevator," Tom says. "Are you going to give up your fitness and good health for the sake of a little giggle?" No way. Press on, joggers. You have nothing to lose but your red faces.

It's wise to do a small measure of advance plotting when you visit a new city. Check out the downtown pollution situation (Tokyo and Mexico City are the worst). Find out where the parks are located. Learn which tenderloins to skirt. Pick up some dope on the most congenial running routes. The best bet for obtaining information is by telephoning a local gym or health club. The Toronto Squash Club, for example, has mapped out two jogging trails through the city, one of five miles' length and the other of three, and the club will make available directions around both trails to visiting joggers. Other clubs in other cities offer the same service. So, in many cases, do local branches of the YMCA and YWCA. They're only a phone call away.

Hotel Rooms

No kidding.

Take a tip from competitive runners who often use hotel corridors to loosen up when they travel to new cities for track meets. Maybe such public carryings-on strike you as too bold, but you can at least settle for running on the spot in the privacy of your hotel room. The trick is to figure out how long you need to jog up and down to reach the desired training effect. One way, probably the most certain, is to count the number of steps you take in the process of covering a mile on your favorite track or through your neighborhood. 2,598 steps to a mile? Okay, equipped with such information, run on the spot until your feet, by count, have come down 2,598 times. It's tedious but scientific. Other on-the-spot joggers use time as a guide. If they cover a mile running at their normal jogging pace in ten minutes and 42 seconds, then they keep an eye on their clocks and they beat on the hotel carpet for the requisite ten minutes and 42 seconds.

Remember, though, that jogging on the spot is a substitute for the real article, a fill-in for emergency and out-of-town occasions. It should be treated as a temporary, now-and-then part of an all-round jogging program. A couple of studies indicate that people who depend on such activities as stationary running, exercycles and other single-spot exercises rarely persevere at their programs. The temptation to watch "All in the Family" while jogging on the spot or to read *Playboy* while exercycling is too tough to resist, and it usually turns out to be one step toward giving up altogether.

Skipping rope, by the way, isn't a bad alternative to jogging on the spot. Pack your rope for trips out of town — but watch your footwork.

Dos and Don'ts

*Practice defensive jogging.
*Remember that indoor tracks are best used as alternatives for bad-weather jogging.
*Shed your inhibitions along with those extra pounds.
*In city or country, plan your jogging route in aavançe.

Heat, Cold, Wind and Rain

*Some days, weather is the jogger's pal.
Other days, it turns into the jogger's
nasty enemy. The secret is to
tell friend from foe and to
equip yourself accordingly.*

T he ideal weather for jogging
is a dry windless day with the temperature in the cozy neighborhood of 50 degrees Fahrenheit (10°C). But any jogger who
confines his workouts to the ideal will find himself at the back
of the jogging class, spending more days cooling it at home
than adding to his running mileage. The goal then is to challenge the elements without going to ridiculous extremes. No
runner should charge into Arctic blasts or battle 50-mile-per-
hour head winds or stagger through jungle heat. Aside from
the extremes, though, almost any day is appropriate for the
prudent jogger to do his thing.

When It's Hot

Kenneth Cooper, the aerobics medicine man, suggests that 98 degrees Fahrenheit is the upward limit for running weather. Dr. Terence Kavanagh cautions his heart-patient joggers to cut back their programs when the temperature passes 80 degrees and to abandon them altogether at past 85 degrees. Harold Gale, an experienced marathoner, 44 years old, collapsed part way through the 1973 Boston Marathon, suffering from heat stroke. Harold Gale died. The temperature that day was 79 degrees Fahrenheit.

Heat, in short, is the trickiest of all elements for joggers to pin down. Hot-weather running can work on the body to cut down blood circulation, thus presenting a heavier burden to the heart. Hot-weather running causes the body to lose water through excessive sweating. Hot-weather running may cause a dangerous drop in blood pressure. And in extreme circumstances — when, for example, marathoners persist through blast-furnace conditions — hot-weather running can induce kidney malfunction and hyperthermia. That's heat stroke, a condition identified by dizziness, dehydration, rapid pulse and breathing, and eventual collapse.

Therefore, accept the consensus of jogging experts and observe the following precautions:

1. For beginning joggers, for those with heart problems, for joggers over 40 or overweight, a top temperature of between 80 and 85 degrees Fahrenheit ought to be the limit, particularly if high humidity accompanies the heat. Kenneth Cooper's 98-degree limit is better suited to well-conditioned runners who are accustomed to warm temperatures.

2. Fuel up on water. A full glass before you set out, and another glass each 15 or 20 minutes will do the trick. Toss in a bit of salt while you're at it, half a pinch to each glass of water. But don't take salt tablets on an empty stomach and don't eat anything with a heavy sugar content. Both can lead to stomach cramps.

3. A fishnet vest makes a sensible top in the heat. It creates an insulating layer of air next to the body and helps reduce its temperature.

4. Remember that it takes a couple of weeks to acclimatize your body to hot temperatures. When the humidity of summer comes on, let yourself ease into the heat, and if you travel to a winter vacation spot, from the frigid north to sunny southern climes, don't rush into your regular jogging schedule. It may take your psyche mere minutes to accept the balmy weather, but your physique needs two weeks to become entirely acclimatized.

5. Cut down your normal program on particularly hot days. Don't run as far or as fast. Tune into your body's messages and pay attention to its tiny whimpers.

When It's Cold

Cold isn't nearly as serious a threat as heat, and in fact, the right clothing can deal with most cold-weather jogging problems. For cold-weather jogging you should invest in the following wardrobe:

—wool fishnet underwear;

—a shirt (preferably turtleneck) for insulation;

—a long-sleeved, hooded sweatshirt made of wool or fleece-lined cotton;

—a windbreaker (cotton poplin, according to many experienced cold-weather running freaks, is best because it allows your sweat to evaporate without condensing on the inside);

—cotton shorts, not a jockstrap (ever tried to straighten a binding jock when you have to plunge your hand through several layers of clothing?);

—long underwear;

—wool or nylon warm-up pants;

—socks and leather or nylon running shoes (waterproof the shoes beforehand, using silicone if they're made of leather);

—mittens (not gloves which are less warming than mitts) preferably made of leather;

—a wool or nylon ski mask that covers head and face.

All dressed? Now get out there and brave the winter's worst. Remember, though, that if you sweat (and you're almost bound to), you must taper off your run slowly in order to avoid a chill. Change out of your clothes immediately after the jog. Don't sit around inviting a bad cold. One more caution: if the underfoot conditions are treacherous, switch to an indoor track. It isn't the cold that is winter's principal weapon against joggers — it's the ice and snow. Rubber-soled running shoes lessen the problem, but when the roads and sidewalks turn to sheets of slippery stuff, there's no sense risking slips and skids, torn ligaments and cracked ankle bones.

When It's Windy

Suppose you weigh 135 pounds. Suppose you're a super runner who can cover a mile in six minutes on a blissfully windless day. Now suppose a wind blows up, nothing of gale force but just a simple ten-mile-per-hour breeze. A test that Dr. Terence Kavanagh has researched indicates that, running in the slight ten-mile wind, you will have to expend six percent more oxygen than you would under windless conditions in order to cover your mile in six minutes. Translated, that means you'd have to run at a pace equal to a sub-five-minute mile.

Wind is deceptive and, for that reason, doubly treacherous. But, like most severe weather conditions, it can be licked by any jogger who sticks to the rules:

1. If you find yourself jogging into a stiff breeze and growing breathless, slow down. Jog at a more leisurely rate. The slower speed combined with the resistance that the wind offers your body will add up to the same training effect as a faster run on a relatively calm day.

2. On those rare occasions when the wind seems to be striking your frame with the force of a cyclone, stop jogging. Walk home. Resume jogging next day.

3. On bearably windy days, when the breeze isn't powerful enough to discourage you, run with the wind in your face at the first stages of the jog and with the wind at your back during the homeward jog. If you attempt the run in the reverse order — with the wind on the outward jog, into the wind on the return jog — you'll have to deal with increased fatigue and perspiration that is turning to cold and icy sweat.

When It's Raining

In a slightly perverse way, many joggers get tremendous satisfaction out of conquering the elements. A three-mile run through a driving rain is in a sense man's equivalent of thumbing his nose at the heavens. Dammit, the jogger says metaphorically, I've licked the worst you can throw at me! The pyschological kick is enormous, and the physical benefits take on the glow of defiance. There's no need to fear a jog through the rain as long as:

1. You keep a closer eye than usual on the road or sidewalk or grassy surface to avoid slips;

2. You dress for the occasion. A water-resistant windbreaker and hat are necessities. Many experienced runners say that nylon is the most useful material for rainy-day jogging wear. If the rain is accompanied by chilly weather, then wear extra clothes in a variation on the winter jogging outfit, always bearing in mind that several layers of light clothing are preferable to a couple of layers of heavy garments.

3. You change out of the wet clothes immediately after the run.

When the Air Is Thin

Planning a trip to Denver? Or to Mexico City? Tibet maybe? Here's a piece of information to keep in mind: when you reach heights of 5,000 feet and up, oxygen is absorbed into your blood and transported to the tissues at a decreased rate. The struggle for oxygen can become fierce, thereby imposing a heavy work load on the heart and respiratory system. It takes from four to six weeks to grow acclimatized to the change in altitude, and during the break-in period the jogger is best advised to cut his program by about 50 percent. Shortness of breath will inevitably overtake the high-altitude runner, but the remedy is simple. Slow down. Catch your breath. Resume jogging at a toned-down pace.

Beware, too, of time changes if you are a globe-hopping jogger. For a couple of days, your mind may be on the west coast but your body is still back on the east coast. You'll notice a disorientation and reduction in energy for as much as 48 or 72 hours while your metabolism makes its tiny adjustments. You will make it easier on yourself if you cut back your customary jogging program by a notch or two.

Dos and Don'ts

*Adapt your jogging — and your jogging equipment — to the weather's fluctuations.
*Don't fight extremes of heat and cold.
*Beware of slippery surfaces.
*Take it easy at high altitudes.
*Don't battle the wind.

The Total Package

Is there more to fitness than jogging?
What about calisthenics, isometrics,
weight-lifting and other forms of exercise? The
curious fact is that some activities benefit areas
of the body that jogging misses while others
may cancel out jogging's hard-won gains.

In the mid-1960s, a Swiss architect named Erwin Weckemann was struck by inspiration and, a persuasive fellow, he prevailed on a local life-insurance firm named Vita to finance turning his revelation into reality. Thus, in Zurich in 1968, the world was blessed with its first Vita Parcours. It was an exercise course spread, in more or less of a circle, over about a mile and a half of parkland with 20 or so exercise stations scattered at intervals around the trail. The idea, according to Weckemann, was for citizens to jog from station to station, pausing only to carry out each of the 20 exercises. The stations were posted with exercise instructions and contained the equipment — bars for chinups, rails for side-way jumps, and so on—needed to carry out the instructions. The system combined play and exercise and fresh air, and in no time at all, Vita Parcours caught on among the Swiss. By the early 1970s, Switzerland boasted 200 of the exercise parks. West Germany had as many, and the idea had begun to spread beyond the continent to the United States and Canada. Vita Parcours had become part of the world's fitness language.

One of the ideas behind Vita Parcours was that jogging alone won't accomplish fitness. It's all very well to jog, Weckemann seemed to be saying, but people need other forms of exercise, specifically calisthenics and isometrics that will get at the muscles jogging overlooks and that will enliven the jogging routine. But how much substance is there in this implied criticism of jogging? Are joggers pursuing a one-dimensional fitness program? Is all the pounding up and down road and track leaving them shortchanged?

Let's examine the evidence.

What Calisthenics Do for You

A daily ten-minute round of exercises, besides serving as an ideal warm-up for a pleasant jog, also improves flexibility, relaxes the body, and prevents muscles from turning loose and flabby. Not bad. But not enough.

"You'd have to hang in at calisthenics for 35 or 40 minutes of straight time in order to get the pulse rate up to a useful level," the fitness director at a San Francisco health club points out. "You'd have to do them awfully fast, too, without any pauses. Even then, you're not going to have a tremendous impact on the cardiovascular system."

That's the consensus among almost all fitness gurus. Sure, the body has 1,030 skeletal muscles and running-jogging can hardly use all of them, but at the same time, calisthenics won't do the job for the heart, lungs and blood that running-jogging performs. You should do calisthenics for the benefits they bestow, but don't imagine that they're a substitute for those hours on the road.

Calisthenics shouldn't be approached in a catch-as-catch-can manner. They have their own built-in rules and priorities.

1. Warm into them gradually. Don't lead off with something tough like a high kick. Begin with jump-ups. Simply hop up and down on the spot 15 or 20 times.

2. Include lots of stretching exercises. For instance: standing upright, feet together and hands at sides, step forward with the left foot, at the same time stretching both arms in front of the body in a reaching motion, then step back bringing the arms backwards as far behind the shoulders as they'll stretch before returning to the starting position and repeating the exercise with the right foot stepping out. This sort of exercise, done five or six times, improves flexibility. It's easy, and fun too, to invent similar stretching drills. Be creative. For inspiration, sporting goods stores, department stores and other agencies carry various calisthenic guides—the standard 5BX and XBX exercise books, for example — at reasonable prices.

3. Don't adopt a program in which all exercises focus on one area of the body. Calisthenics should benefit muscles in the back, abdomen, shoulders and arms (jogging takes care of the legs), and the mix of exercises ought to contain something for every area with perhaps a little extra for your weak spots.

What Isometrics Do for You

You remember isometrics. Big fad in the 1950s and 1960s and still around today. Supposed to develop instant muscles. Take up isometrics and turn into an overnight Charles Atlas.

Only needs a few minutes a day. Do it in your own room. For example: sit in a chair, place your hands under the seat, attempt to lift the legs of the chair off the ground. That's isometrics. Pushing a car out of a snow drift is also isometrics. So is bending over to lift a dead weight, like an overpacked trunk. So, for that matter, is a chinup. Or a pushup.

What happens when you do an isometric exercise is that you contract a muscle without moving any of the limbs—a leg, an arm, an ankle — that the muscle is attached to. No joint budges in the course of an isometric exercise. When you try to lift the chair you're sitting on, three things occur: the chair doesn't budge, your elbow doesn't bend, your bicep muscle contracts but doesn't shorten. The action, carried out on a regular basis, molds beautifully blooming biceps, the sort that woo the girls on the beach and scare away the bullies. Nice, in short, for cosmetic purposes. But of little benefit to the organs that count: the heart, the lungs, and the circulatory system.

The action of an ismoetric exercise, in fact, places pressure on the heart. For people who already suffer from coronary problems, an isometric flexing can be positively hazardous. That's the word from Dr. Terence Kavanagh, who points out that "straining ... may well build the body beautiful. But the isometric element involved makes it an avocation suitable only for those with the healthiest of cardiovascular systems."

Kenneth Cooper doesn't think that even those people with healthy cardiovascular systems should fool around with isometrics. Such exercises, he says, have no improving effect on the oxygen-distributing system, don't add power to the heart and don't strengthen the lungs.

If you've been laid up in bed or otherwise idle, you might try a mild round of isometrics to tighten up deteriorating muscles, but don't make them a regular part of your exercise program.

What Weight-lifting Does for You

Shirley Patterson is a remarkable woman. She started skydiving when she was 36 — that was in 1972 — and started weight-lifting a couple of years before that. By 1976, she was on her own managing the North Hollywood Health Club in California. She was bench-pressing 125 pounds. She was weight-lifting 170-pound barbells. She was five-feet-two and weighed 112 pounds. She was gorgeous.

In a letter written near the end of August of '76, she explained the secret of her good looks. "My main interest is total physical fitness, which is a combination of strength, endurance, flexibility and co-ordination. I lift very heavy weights in my workouts, which is great for strength and building a nice body, but it doesn't give me the endurance I need. I get this from running. Running helps to stretch out and elongate the muscles, which is almost the complete opposite to what weight training does. The combination of weight training and running keeps my body healthy and more shapely."

That's one view on the subject of weight-lifting; it isn't confined to the persuasive Miss Patterson but is shared by many track coaches who advocate lifting. But there's also the opposing view, championed to a large degree by Dr. Kenneth Cooper, that there is something counter-productive about combining two such disparate activities as jogging and weight-lifting. The object of running and jogging is to build up the oxygen-carrying system and to make the flow of oxygen to all the body's tissues more efficient. What happens in weight-lifting is that new tissue is created. Lifting weights builds large, knotty muscles which place an extra load on the oxygen-transport system. So much new tissue to service! It hardly seems fair to the heart and blood vessels.

These two opposing views on weight-lifting can probably be reconciled by taking the middle road. For dedicated joggers (those who are sticking to their programs over a lengthy period), weight-lifting in moderation (not more than one hour per week) can offer extra dividends. Never mind championship bench presses, clean-and-jerks and the like. That's not for joggers. Their use of weights makes sense when it's intended to improve the strength of muscles that relate to their jogging. Thus, lifting weights in ways that build up the shoulder muscles and the muscles at the back of the neck is beneficial because such muscular development encourages more effective posture and breathing during a jog.

In the same way, power work with gymnasium machines that strengthen the abdominal, hip, thigh and calf muscles work in favor of the jogger.

There are two problems in carrying out this muscle-building program. First, to get the maximum advantage out of a modest weight-lifting plan, an ambitious jogger would need access to a well-equipped gymnasium. Secondly, the weight-lifting jogger must not overdo his weight-lifting. Anyone who finds his desire for the muscles that lifting weights produces supplanting his affection for jogging is asking for trouble. His heavily developed muscles with all their new tissue could over-strain the hard-working oxygen-transport system.

What Yoga Does for You

Yoga has a sissy image, something for wives and for eccentrics who dig sitar music, vegetarian restaurants and the smell of incense. That seems a shame because the fact is that yoga is excellent for all-round flexibility and may be just the ticket as a supplement to jogging. Competitive runners who have taken up yoga report that it also acts as an impressive relaxing agent and encourages erect posture and stronger powers of concentration. One such disciple, an experienced California marathoner named Ian Jackson, has written that with yoga "I freed not only my legs from soreness but my entire body. I realized new-found pleasure in simple movement. I was light on my feet. My limbs swung freely and easily. I had an incredible feeling of weightlessness and vitality ... "

Good news, but, alas, there's also bad news. It has nothing to do the validity of yoga, which seems beyond question, but with the difficulty in approaching it, let alone in mastering it. Yoga is a Hindu philosophy was well as a Hindu system of exercises, and the exercises are aimed at asserting control over the mind and the body. Almost by definition, yoga movements are complex; they set out to accomplish nothing less than the precise stretching of each of the body's muscles. Needless to say, it requires the dedication of years for a yoga practitioner to attain the perfection of Indian yogis.

Where does this situation leave the humble jogger? Well, he could, for starters, take a crack at one of the basic yoga positions. Sit on a thick rug or sleeping bag or some other comfortable floor covering. Cross legs and bend knees to a point about eight or nine inches above the floor. Rest hands on knees. Hold an upright posture, back as straight as possible. Relax legs.

Allow weight of arms to lean on legs without pressing or forcing. Let knees sink to floor.

That's the drill, and in even so simple a movement, the limbs resist, uttering tiny cries. It's hard, and if such a basic yoga position is difficult, imagine what the more complex movements are like.

There are two ways for the humble jogger to get into yoga. First, by studying an illustrated yoga manual and practicing the movements on his own. Secondly, by enrolling in a yoga class, a phenomenon that has multiplied in church basements, YMCAs, fitness clubs and other such organizations all over the world in the 1970s. The trouble with the first suggestion is that, even when the book is as explicitly detailed as *Be Young with Yoga* by Richard Hittleman or *Yoga Self-Taught* by Andre Van Lysebeth (both of which are readily available and widely praised), an initiate is easily led into error. A small deviation can cancel the intention of a given yoga movement. A jogger who's serious about yoga is probably best advised to learn from a teacher who's already taken the time to master the system's secrets. Then, back home in his very own ashram, he can practice the movements. Ease his flexibility. Feel relaxed. Concentrate. And take his new loose, erect body out for a jog.

Dos and Don'ts

*Choose exercises that tone up your weakest muscle areas.
*Don't forget that over-developed muscles can strain your oxygen-transport system.
*Yoga holds the secret to increased flexibility.

Jogging and the Inner Life

Will jogging sharpen your thinking?
Speed up your brain processes? Ease
depression? Cure anxiety? Improve sleep?
The answer in every case appears
to be a loud yes.

In late 1976, a curious and kind of thrilling story line leaped off the cover of *New Times*, the investigative magazine published in New York City. "Getting High On Running," the cover line read, and inside the magazine, the story was titled "Running: The New High." Running? In the age of drugs and sex and violence and booze and other wonders calculated to elevate the senses, if not to blow the mind entirely, in this post-psychedelic era, *running* is a high?

New Times claimed it was so, and the magazine marshalled impressive evidence to back up its statements. There was a diagnosis of the "third wind" that may occur after thirty minutes of steady running, a state during which there is "a sudden release of creative energies and fantasies ... akin to some of the mystical states, like meditation or Zen." There were reports of successes achieved by psychiatrists who prescribed regular sessions of jogging and running for alcoholics and chronic smokers and drug addicts, patients who found the strength to beat their problems on the track. And there were interviews with runners who sang of the euphoria of their miles on the run. "Running," according to one trendy fellow who spoke to *New Times*, "is where it's happening. Running is getting to know yourself. It's better than alcohol, better than drugs. Sometimes, I swear, it's better than sex."

Ah, jogging and the inner life, jogging and mental health, jogging and brain power. The proof of the connection, according to *New Times* and other authorities, is all around us. And we don't even have to rely on contemporary sources. Consider the Bible, the Book of Daniel, 12: 4, "Many shall run to and fro and knowledge shall be increased."

Well, maybe that's going too far. Running and jogging are hardly likely to convert a dummy into a wizard, a devil into a saint (or vice versa), an Edith Bunker into a Barbara Walters. But what jogging is apt to do is free Edith Bunker to be more splendidly herself. Jogging cannot create brains and talents where they haven't previously existed. What jogging can accomplish, it's been established, is sharpen wits, focus attention, calm the inner furies and generally encourage a mental state that is conducive to a jogger's most productive intellectual and emotional capacities. Jogging can be a catalyst. And a cheerleader.

There are a couple of caveats to be noted in connection with this magical process. One is that it isn't immediate or easily earned. At the beginning of a jogging program, the newcomer must concentrate on his body's problems in adapting to the unfamiliar activity. The mind has time only to wonder how in the world it and the body are going to survive. The other caveat is simply that the whole process shouldn't be overrated. "What I can't stand," says Frank Shorter, the great American marathoner, "is these guys who make a cult out of running. It ruins the whole thing to take it too seriously." Still, once the non-physical benefits of jogging are placed in perspective and once the jogger has been at his task long and faithfully enough (three or four months of steady sessions at a very minimum three or four times a week), then he has opened himself to potential rewards that have less to do with the feet and heart and more to do with the head and soul.

Jogging to Expand the Mind

Jogging leaves the mind with time to think. That's obvious. What isn't obvious, not to non-joggers at any rate, is that the thinking becomes focused to an astonishing degree. "Minutiae and trivia recede into the background," Dr. Terence Kavanagh writes from personal running experience, "leaving only the important high points for consideration." Erich Segal says that in the course of several runs he wrote the first chapter of *Love Story*. An American criminal lawyer, recounting some of his jogging experiences in a 1975 runners' magazine, claims he framed the outlines for his best jury addresses in mid-jog. The act of running, it's plain, stimulates the brain, and offers some runners a variety of mental experiences in the space of one jog. Gary Ross, a Canadian novelist, gives a description of his mental reactions that seems typical of this phenomenon: "When I get locked into a running rhythm, I divert myself by rewriting troublesome sentences and paragraphs. Never anything more grand—I keep to the nuts and bolts of the novel when in motion. After a mile and a half, I'm unable to direct my mind. I blank out, start singing a song which has the same time signature as my feet—maybe 'Free Man in Paris' by Joni Mitchell. The running then becomes a contest between the beat and my capacity for lifting one foot and then the other with sufficient haste."

The mental high and the rush of the creative juices that usually occur after 30 or 40 minutes of running may owe their origins to something called a "third wind." That's the speculation of Dr. George Sheehan, the New Jersey cardiologist and runner. "What I find," he says, "is that for the creative thinker — which is what I basically am — you begin to see analogies between things that are incongruous, which I think is the essence of creativity. You get ideas that you don't get driving a car or sitting at a desk. I think you're the best you can be out there during this third wind. It doesn't always happen, and when it doesn't running can be a drag. You may end up with a grocery list, but you may also start thinking about a problem that has been bothering you and it becomes clearer to you. The third wind sort of puts you in a different world, a kingdom if you will."

But suppose on a particular day you don't enter the kingdom. Suppose you end up with a shopping list. No need to despair. If you experience no increase in your brain power during a long jog, you may still reap mental benefits in your post-jog hours. Many regular joggers experience what a California exercise physiologist terms "a concentration carry-over from the run." That is to say, the joggers find their runs have cleared their minds of clutter and cobwebs and enabled them to concentrate more efficiently on the essentials of their tasks. "My joggers," the physiologist says, "report that, to a man, they have functioned better at their jobs in the year after they started jogging than in the year before. I don't think it's a coincidence."

Neither does the Department of Kinesiology at the University of Waterloo in Canada, which launched in 1974 a four-year study, the most comprehensive ever undertaken in North America, of the effects of a regular exercise program on 100 employees in middle-managment positions. The employees ranged in age from 23 to 62, and, in the succinct words of the study's director, "They matched the overall average fitness in Canada: lousy." They rose above this level as they pursued their exercise program, which emphasized jogging, and at the same time, according to preliminary assessments of the study, the employees improved to a measurable degree in "mental alertness, memory, personality and emotional stability." Why? The projected answer is that exercise encourages an increase in blood supply to the brain which, in turn, quickens the worker's mental processes. Simple — and for joggers, oh so reassuring.

Jogging to Relieve Tension

"World-class distance runners," according to Bill Morgan, a psychologist from the University of Wisconsin, "are all lower than the general population in the incidence of psychological problems that result from tension and anxiety."

Jogging is not a mental cure-all, but it does help work off tension and creates a feeling of well-being that carries over into other areas of the jogger's life. For those who suffer from acid in the stomach, which can cause irritableness, jogging offers non-medicinal relief. The same goes for the digestive track; joggers, believe it or not, are much less constipated than non-joggers. Perhaps most essentially, jogging builds up the physical stamina that's vital to head off emotional trauma. Jogging won't save you from cataclysmic events — wars will continue to darken the scene and so will divorces, traffic jams and importuning relatives — but it will help strengthen your ability to weather crises intact.

Tex Maule put the relationship between jogging and tension in neat perspective in his book, *Running Scarred*: "Although jogging is not an unalloyed pleasure, it does have a very pleasant side effect. I can't think of anything that relaxes you more mentally or eases tension more completely than a leisurely run. While you are running, you do not worry about anything. It is an all-absorbing occupation, and when you have finished, the pleasant fatigue combined with the sense of accomplishment keeps tension away for a long time."

The Jogger's Self-Image

Secretly, in the part of him that's most hidden away, how does a jogger see himself?

Easy question.

Answer: As Gary Cooper on a dusty street facing down the Clanton Brothers. As the last maverick. As a primeval force challenging anything that moves on wheels. As a one-man triumph over masochism. As an independent soul. As someone apart and special.

Make no mistake, the boost to the ego that every daydreaming jogger experiences is almost as bracing as the more measurable blessings to the heart and respiratory system. "The first time you complete five or six miles, no matter what the speed," Dr. Terence Kavanagh has noted, "you know you have set yourself apart from the majority of your fellow men." The fellow with the humble beginner's pace of 50-yard walk followed by a 50-yard jog, back home in 15 minutes, is bound to experience a sense of self-esteem almost equal to the dazzling emotions of the guy who knocks off five miles before breakfast every other morning. The sense of accomplishment is democratic. It's also a renewable resource.

"You can feel you're getting something important done every day you run," Frank Shorter has said. "You have the tangible sense of doing something significant."

Jogging and the Good Sleep

Sleep habits sometimes seem almost as personal as fingerprints. No two people, even two married people, follow identical sleep patterns. Jogging isn't going to change sleeping's idiosyncratic nature. Different people will find the length and depth and quality of their sleep changing in different ways as they get into jogging programs. Some joggers, for example, report that after a year or more of steady workouts, they can get by on fewer hours of sleep each night; they used to need a regular eight, now six is enough to set them up for a solid day of activity. Others find that the extra energy they use in two- and three-mile jogs means that they must be in bed by 11 o'clock to ensure their vitality on the job next day.

Among all the varying reactions, however, one fact is certain: jogging—indeed any form of cardiovascular exercise—almost guarantees a sounder and more consistent night's sleep. Exercise, it's clear, strengthens the body and the vital organs and makes them better prepared to withstand attacks of emotional stress, and their accompanying tension. Since it's this demon, emotional stress, that probably more than any other single factor gets in the way of sound sleep, exercise, especially jogging, holds the potential key to a restful night and a productive next day.

No scientists have yet definitively analyzed the impact of exercise on sleep, but it seems probable that exercise lengthens the Delta phase of sleep and shortens the Alpha phase. The Delta phase is the deepest sleep that predominates during the first half of any period while the Alpha phase, during which most dreaming occurs, comes at the end of a rest period. With more Delta, you're apt to arise feeling refreshed, and with more jogging, you're apt to experience more Delta. It's almost as simple as that.

Metabolic activity patterns are another major factor in sleep patterns. Dr. S. B. Whitehead in his book, *Facts on Sleep*, decided that people fall into one of three predominant rhythms. There's the morning type who begins the day in high gear and slows down during the afternoon until he's wiped out at night. There's the evening type who staggers through the morning and finds himself in superb spirits by evening. And there's the lucky type with the metabolism that puts him in solid condition in both morning and evening with only a mild let-down in the early afternoon. Each of these types, Whitehead suggests, should adopt different sleep habits. The morning fellow is best advised to stick with the traditional "early to bed, early to rise" routine while the evening man ought to do just the opposite — get to the office late and continue work into the evening. Each of the types might also squeeze in a nap during the time period most appropriate to his metabolic condition. The perfect guy, the one who experiences only a brief slump at mid-day, should take 30 minutes' rest after lunch. The morning man might nap before dinner, the evening man should stretch his sleep into the nine a.m. to 10:30 a.m. range. Obviously it makes good sense to adapt your jogging times to your own metabolic pattern.

One warning: many joggers, feeling cocky about their new vitality, deliberately cut down on sleeping hours. That may work for some people, especially under-40s joggers, but most physiologists warn against cheating on sleep. "The occasional late night is inevitable," writes Terence Kavanagh, "but don't make a habit of it and expect to reap the benefits of training."

Dos and Don'ts

*Let jogging free your creative energies.
*Look to jogging to upgrade your self-esteem.
*Don't skimp on sleep.

The Body's Whimpers and Cries

Jogging brings pains with its rewards.
It can hurt —and it can threaten muscles,
limbs and organs with special dangers.
Still, a little preparation and
a lot of precaution can head
off most of the hazards and
cancel out most of the pain.

"Everything that doesn't destroy you," the German philospher Friedrich Wilhelm Nietzsche once said, "makes you stronger."

According to historical records, Nietzsche was not a jogger, but his philosophy, at least as it's reflected in the above fragment, is one that twentieth-century joggers might profit by. Jogging is hardly a test by fire. It does, however, serve up a share of pain, and those who take up the pastime must expect to endure a small share of grief.

Jogging's Pains

In the matter of pain and injuries, joggers will find nothing but discouraging words from two very different quarters. First, the marathoners who represent the pinnacle of jogging-running success offer little comfort. And, second, medical men who are down on jogging suggest that such an idiotic activity no doubt lies at the bottom of every world sorrow from pimples to the breakdown in relations between Russia and Albania.

"There are moments of such torture and helplessness," Bruce Kidd, the Canadian distance runner, has written of his mental and physical state during a run, "that you'd turn your mother into the Gestapo if only they'd allow you to stop." Then there's Frank Shorter, the Olympic marathoner from the US and his catalog of troubles: hammer toes, blood in the urine and cramps in the liver, a byproduct of a sugar deficiency in the blood called hypoglycemia which is common among marathoners. So it goes. But there are two arguments that joggers can marshall in reply. The first is that both Kidd and Shorter, as well as most other complaining runners, have continued to run, and they're running as much for pleasure as for competition. The second is that joggers and marathoners, despite the daydreams of the former, are two different breeds. Joggers, not as compulsive, gifted or single-minded as the competitive long-distance runners, jog simply to stay fit, and thus their more limited mileage is unlikely to expose them to the exotic ailments and terrors that afflict Kidd and Shorter.

Now for the doctors. "Jogging," says Dr. Joseph Beninson of Detroit's Henry Ford Hospital, "squashes your spine like an accordion." "Jogging," says Dr. Don Lannin, physician to the Minnesota Viking football team, "has too much bang-bang and that is particularly damaging to the hip." "Among the casualties of jogging," writes Dr. J.E. Schmidt in *Playboy* magazine "are the 'dropped' stomach, the loose spleen, the floating kidney and the fallen arches."

Enough, enough. There may be a measure of truth in such warnings. Nothing physical, after all, is utterly fail-safe. But the majority of claims against jogging are at least premature. By the mid-1970s, few adequate studies had been carried out to

determine whether jogging is detrimental. "The relatively recent avalanche of middle-aged persons joining the ranks of
joggers and marathon runners," a report in the *New York
Times* noted in the autumn of 1976, "has resulted in research
studies in many countries, that, as yet, give no clear indication
of the lasting health benefits or risks that result from regular
strenuous exercise programs for well persons." The jury, in
short, hasn't yet rendered its verdict in the jogging case.

What is known, of course, is that hundreds of thousands of
men and women who have taken to jogging report improved
health, especially improved cardiovascular health. And what
is also known is that, for most joggers, the chances of injury
are enormously reduced by following sensible jogging procedures. Warming up before a jog. Warming down after the jog.
Wearing proper equipment. Never overtaxing individual capacities. Lavishing love and care on the feet. The aches and pains
may not be entirely absent, but the percentages for avoiding
serious or lasting troubles are cut to a manageable margin
when joggers observe safety tips like the following:

1. Warm up gradually. It's the cold rush into a jog that often
inflicts injury on unprepared, unloosened limbs.

2. Make certain you've put on your shoes to the proper fit.
Smooth wrinkles out of the socks. Lace shoes snugly. Test for
flex and comfort. Feel right? Jog off. Feel wrong? Undress your
feet and begin again, switching socks if necessary or laces or
even shoes until they feel right.

3. Never run in an up and down style. Thump, thump. Bang,
bang. That'll bring on bruises to the heel and pain to the legs
and spine. Thump, thump. Crack goes the knee. Bang, bang.
Tinkle goes the spine. Then the heel. Then the ankle. So long
jogging. Hello, hospital.

4. Don't panic. For many joggers, the toughest part of the
jog comes in the first few minutes. That's when shin bones
and other parts of the physical apparatus react to the fresh
activity with a few whimpers. The breath might come a bit
sluggishly, too. Other signals crop up in distant parts of your
frame, all with the same message: is this trip truly necessary?
Pay no attention—unless, of course, you note some vivid and
absolutely unmistakeable sign of deep trouble. But, for the

most part, pay no attention and don't let the body's complaints, as it shakes off its apathy, panic you into quitting.

5. Try exercises that strengthen the hamstrings, which are
the tendons at the back of the legs near the knee. They're a
frequent location for injury. Stretching exercises are good for
hamstrings. Fitness expert Allan Scott has a simple exercise
that he suggests will increase hamstring strength: "A weighted
boot or something heavy that can be tied to the foot is ideal for
working just the hamstrings. Simply attach the boot or weight,
stand beside a door for support and slowly raise the weight up
behind you by bending at the knee. Lift the weight as high as
possible and then lower slowly to the floor. Perform three sets
of 15 repetitions on each leg." Bent knee situps also
strengthen the hamstrings.

6. Got the sniffles? Sore throat? Feel a cold coming on?
Don't jog until you're cured. Then take it easy when you
return to action. Jogging during any sickness intensifies the
ailment and interferes with the jog's benefits.

7. Bill Bowerman suggests that if you suffer from any sort of
muscle cramps and spasms while you're jogging, a little extra
salt in your food might solve the problem, provided you're not
on a salt-free diet.

8. Shin splints are a painful nuisance. What produces them
is a sort of tearing of the tissue next to the shin bones. Check
your shoes — they may, for reasons of bad fit or insufficient
padding on the heels, lie at the root of the trouble. Switch to a
softer jogging surface — a change from cement to grass may
ease the pain. Or else take a couple of days off. Stretching
exercises can head off shin splints, especially exercises in
which you flex your feet with weights centered over the toes.
Stretching exercise that get at the back of the legs — the
hamstrings and Achilles tendons — also seem to benefit the
front of the legs where shin splints occur. For the most part,
shin splints are a mystery. Sometimes they seem to ease in
intensity in mid-jog. Sometimes they linger for long periods,
not severe enough to cripple but just enough to annoy.

9. On the appearance of extreme or persistent pain in the
regions of the arms, chest, neck, head, ears or upper abdomen,
stop and report to a doctor. Follow the same course of action

in case of dizziness or shortness of breath. All are possible symptoms of circulatory problems.

10. Don't fool around with a bad back. If you're prone to low back pain or sciatica, if there is something wrong with a disk in your back—degeneration or rupture—then check the advice of an orthopedist. There's a chance, sorry about this, that jogging may not be your game.

11. Psyche yourself. That's one way to block out nagging aches and pains that aren't portents of anything crippling. Bill Morgan, the University of Wisconsin psychologist who studied the group of champion distance runners, reported as follows: "I found that these men all used a cognitive strategy to dissociate from pain. For example, one man will imagine himself building a house—from drafting the plans, pouring the foundation, doing the plumbing, the framing, every shingle. As the race ends, he's admiring the landscape. Another mentally puts on a stack of Beethoven records and runs the whole way to changing symphonies." And so on. Naturally the humble jogger isn't about to subject himself to the physical turmoils of a seasoned marathon runner, but in his smaller way, he can still make use of the "cognitive-strategy" method of holding his pains at bay.

12. Be reasonably wary of small indoor tracks. Many of the newer models have cement bases that can be tough on ankles and knees. The constant whirling around a miniscule oval—24 laps to the mile—also offers possibilities of damage to the delicate mechanism of the inner-ear balance. If a small track seems a threat in any of these ways, look for roomier quarters.

13. On those occasions when business, sickness, circumstance or plain laziness take you away from your regular jogging schedule, don't pick up the schedule where you dropped off. That's asking for trouble. Break in with gradual ease. Cut back on the distance and speed of your jog. Your body won't be prepared for the old schedule, and the strain of reaching for it after a layoff will result in pain.

14. Keep a gentle governor on yourself. Plenty of troubles arise when joggers load their jogs with too much stress and strain and striving. Such effort is part of the syndrome that says an activity's real worth is measured by the amount of

suffering it incurs. Wrong. There's much more sense in the words of Tom Osler, a teacher of mathematics at an American college and an experienced distance runner: "When we feel good, look good and are alert and productive, our bodies will be adapting effectively to stresses, like running, which we place upon them. If we feel tired, pain and are washed out, we need rest, not stress."

15. Achilles tendons—the tendons above your heel—occasionally develop pains. The relief? Check the heels on your track shoes. If they're too low or too hard, you may have found the source of your miseries. Check your arch supports. If you have none, get some fitted because arches and Achilles tendons are interconnected. Exercises for the Achilles are essential, too, exercises that stre-e-e-etch the tendons as much as you can sensibly stand.

16. Be flexible. Don't pursue a schedule with religious faith if it's leaving you consistently wiped out. Forget the zeal and adopt commonsense. It may be that the schedule you've locked yourself in to is much too demanding for your fitness level. Cut back until you arrive at a program that yields the sense of well-being you're looking for.

17. Don't, as a general rule for joggers over 40 and for many joggers under that age, run after a tiring night when you've had less than your regular sleep. This places a strain on the heart.

18. When some smug fellow points out that a friend of his, only 39 and strong as a horse, dropped dead of heart failure in the middle of a jog on a peaceful sunny day, you should recall the words of an anonymous doctor and jogger who wrote in a 1971 issue of an American magazine called *Fitness For Living* that, "No fitness program is entirely without risk, especially in those aged 40 or over. But, for that matter, neither is any medication—and exercise is a form of therapy—completely harzard free. A simple aspirin may do you in."

19. If all else fails, recall the words of Fyodor Dostoevsky: "Suffering is the sole origin of consciousness."

Dos and Don'ts

*Count on mild pain as an occasional jogging companion. Call a doctor if your pain is more than mild or more than occasional.

*Don't compete with your body.

*Remember that the first line of defense against pain and injury is commonsense.

Cigarettes, Booze and the Jogger's Menu

Should joggers change their eating habits?
Their drinking and smoking habits?
The answers are probably yes,
but what are the reasons and what
are the changes?

There can't be many joggers, none over the age of 12 anyway, who haven't already absorbed the message about booze, cigarettes and junk foods. They're bad for the health, and they make people unfit. What many joggers may not realize is that after the initial ego-gratification of jogging has worn off, it is diet that will keep the jogger on track. An unfit jogger who indulges in too much alcohol, tobacco, and too many non-nutritious calories will soon be too tired to keep up with the race and will quit, the victim of a bad diet as well as poor fitness.

Some runners, like Wilma Rudolph, manage to give excellent

performances on a diet of hot dogs, hamburgers and soda pop. But their performance time is short, intended to win in competition, while the ordinary jogger's major goal is long-range fitness. For some joggers, the advice of French long-distance runner Michael Jazy may suffice: "An athlete in shape is like a pregnant woman. You may indulge your tastes, but be sure not to overdo." However, it is important to know which foods are nutritious and which contain empty calories. The jogger interested in his health will aim for a diet which chooses nutritious foods and eliminates the others. He may have to borrow on the same self-discipline which gets him up at 6 a.m. for a run around the track—and recognize that following a sensible diet is as important as running that extra lap.

The Case Against Alcohol

A survey conducted by an international track organization in 1975 disclosed that one out of every three competitive runners around the world enjoys imbibing of the grape. Marathoner Frank Shorter admits that he enjoys his beer and stunned purists by spending the night before the 1972 Olympic marathon drinking with his wife. He explains it, saying, "I was trying to forget how much I'd suffer once I started to run." However, the point of jogging is not to endure suffering, but to build up better exercise tolerance and a healthier body — gradually. Both these goals are hindered by the effect of alcohol on the system.

For a start, alcohol is high in calories, useless calories that provide no nutrition and even worse, may make the drinker cut down on important nutrients to avoid gaining weight. For those jogging to lose weight, a slow process in any case, alcohol should be avoided as much as possible, in any form: beer, wine or booze.

For everyone, alcohol prevents the absorption of several B vitamins, and a vitamin deficiency could occur, slowing the runner's progress. The liver requires protein and certain vitamins and minerals to burn off alcohol in the body, so it is particularly important to replace those used up nutrients, but this causes an additional consumption of calories and consequent weight gain.

Because alcohol moves into the bloodstream it can inhibit the flow of oxygen to the body's tissues and muscles, including the heart. This slows the runner down, physically and mentally, and cancels out the boost jogging should give the cardiovascular system. Jogging with alcohol in the system is difficult, and pretty soon the drinking jogger abandons his jogging program in favor of another relaxing cocktail. So much for fitness.

Despite the effects of alcohol on the system, few people who drink now will give it up to jog. It is true that joggers who drink will become more fit than if they didn't jog, but they'd reach an even healthier state if they went on the wagon or cut back to a low or moderate level of drinking. At any rate, there are two rules that are indisputable concerning the relationship between alcohol and jogging:

1. Don't jog while under the spell of drink. The alcohol puts a strain on your heart and reduces your judgement of speed, distance and endurance.

2. Don't jog with a hangover. The booze still in your system will cause you to tire more quickly and generally sabotage your performance.

The Case Against Smoking

Formula: One non-smoker's jog = three smoker's jogs.

To get the fitness benefit, a smoker must work three times as hard as a non-smoker. Carbon monoxide is the reason. When a smoker inhales on a cigarette, he takes in particles of carbon monoxide. These particles push aside the oxygen from the molecules of hemoglobin in the red blood cells and create a deficiency of oxygen in the circulatory system, thereby cancelling the most important benefit of jogging.

Smoking is also detrimental to the jogger in the long run. The smoker's lungs become clogged with residue, lowering his oxygen intake and rendering his circulatory system less efficient. It becomes harder and harder to breathe, particularly when exercising. Note the person who is winded after climbing only one or two flights of stairs: chances are he's a long-term smoker. The smoking jogger will get discouraged more quickly when he sees his non-smoking neighbor continue running long after he himself is out of wind. It's a good reason to quit — smoking that is. Although willing to confess to drinking, few professional athletes will admit that they smoke; and all recognize that smoking and serious competition don't mix. Don't use a cigarette as a reward at the end of a jog. Find another way of patting yourself on the back, one that's less harmful to your health.

Non-smoking joggers face some of the hazards of the smoking jogger when they run in urban areas. Inhaling carbon monoxide from car exhausts has the same effect as smoking. It has been estimated that a person living in a major urban center inhales the equivalent of a pack of cigarettes a day. However, the hazards can be reduced if the jogger is careful.

1. Run upwind from cars whenever possible.
2. Try to run at least a block away from busy city streets.
3. Never jog in the midst of traffic. If necessary find a park, even if it means a little extra traveling time.

The Jogger's Diet

Most professional athletes are always searching for the perfect food or the perfect diet, and in the end many tend to rely on fads. Long-distance runner Lasse Viren claims reindeer milk was the key to his two Olympic gold medals. Australian track coach Percy Cerutty feeds his runners fresh fruit, stale bread, figs, nuts and dates. Others claim that anything from onions to wheat germ will win a race. Marathon runners in particular have designed a diet which provides an extra kick at the end of a race.

The diet, commonly known as carbohydrate overload, is followed by many marathon runners. Fifty percent of the runners finishing under three hours at a 1974 Trail's End Marathon in Seaside, Oregon, used it. Marathoner Jerome Drayton believes in it, as does Bruce Kidd, a Canadian long-distance runner. "You pig it up," Bruce Kidd writes, "on all the pasta, cake and ice cream you can get your hands on." For those who have long been told that starch is fattening and to be avoided, and have an insatiable sweet tooth it sounds ideal. But wait ...

The diet is based on the fact that carbohydrates build up the body stores of the most easily converted fuel, glycogen. During the first three days of the six-day diet the athlete eats a high-protein, high-fat diet to deplete the body of excess glycogen, forcing the body to begin producing its own from its stores of protein. During the three days before the race the saturation begins. The athlete avoids most protein and fat and eats masses of carbohydrates: pizza, bread and fruit. The body converts the carbohydrates to glycogen, which is then added to the glycogen already produced, giving a rebound effect.

Studies have shown that the muscles contain up to eight times their normal amount of glycogen and provide two to three times the normal exercise tolerance. For marathoners aiming at running more than 26 miles in under three hours easily available fuel is necessary, with enough left over for the extra kick.

For joggers, running a mile a day the carbohydrate diet has no beneficial effects and a few detrimental ones. It cannot be kept up indefinitely without ruining the health, since everybody needs protein and fats to fuel their body. The jogger wants to make jogging part of his day, but his day should never be centered around his jog and that includes his diet. In other words, jogging should help you have more energy, not less. In addition, the carbohydrate diet adds calories which the body will not consume. Jogging is not an efficient way to lose weight; a 170-pound man will only consume 157 calories if he runs 1.5 miles in eight minutes. If the jogger jogs 1.5 miles in 16 minutes only 175 calories are consumed, not enough to burn up the extra carbohydrates. The message is clear for joggers: stay away from the marathoners' trick.

In the same way, joggers should steer clear of most other offbeat ways of meddling with food intake, including such get-thin-quick devices as diet pills, appetite suppressants, water pills and hormone injections. None offers long-term answers to good health, and many are harmful. An unbalanced diet not only doesn't provide enough fuel for the jogger to continue his program with enthusiasm, but it can also cause a vulnerability to viruses and infections that interrupt the jogging program. Canada's marathoner at the 1976 Olympics, Jerome Drayton, claims his diet of meat and fish for three days weakened him to the point that he caught a cold, hindering his performance.

It is also important not to listen to old wives' tales about avoiding certain foods when running. Drinking moderate amounts of water will not add to weight, nor will milk. The only special precaution a jogger should take is making sure salt and water lost during jogging are replaced. It is an easy task, drinking a cup of bouillon will take care of most people. Bouillon has few calories and quickly replaces lost water and salt.

No one is asking you to eat like long-distance runner Paavo Nurmi, who became a vegetarian and gave up sweets, hard liquor, coffee and tea, although it certainly wouldn't hurt you. Instead, learn what foods provide nutrition with the fewest calories and least stress on the heart and the rest of the decision is up to you.

What is a nutritious diet? Very simply it is a balanced combination of carbohydrates, fats and proteins. Despite the previous warning about a high-carbohydrate diet, carbohydrates should make up about 60 percent of calories consumed. Fats should comprise 30 percent and protein 10 percent. However, simply measuring in terms of calorie percentages can be misleading. It is important that the calories consumed be worthwhile nutritionally. Eating cake and other sugars for the carbohydrate portion will provide the body with no nutrition and put an additional strain on the heart.

Carbohydrates

Carbohydrates come in many forms, including potatoes and bread, the two items most commonly eliminated from reducing diets. However, vegetables, fruits and sugar (both raw, white and honey) also contain carbohydrates. Of the group, only sugar, in any form, has nothing to offer nutritionally and could be completely eliminated from the diet.

Despite the myth that sugar is "quick energy", it takes as much time as any other carbohydrate to be turned into fuel. While Chris Evert continues to take honey to the tennis courts to give her a lift, there is no need for the jogger to have any form of quick energy. His diet should be sufficient to carry him through his paces, with enough left over for a full day's activities.

Whole-grain breads and potatoes, are a valuable source of nutrition and should not be removed from the diet. Fresh, unprocessed fruits and vegetables also provide vital carbohydrates to the body without adding unnecessary quantities of sugar. It is true that carbohydrates add pounds, but only if eaten in excess of amounts needed by the body, so don't give them up. Instead choose wisely and limit the amount, as you should limit all food intake.

Protein

In a word association game, the word protein would most commonly be put with meat, particularly steak. But steak is only one of the forms of protein, and not necessarily the best.

Ancient Greek athletes trained on vegetables, figs, meal-cakes and cheese, with meat as a relish. Meat in the diet of an athlete became popular in the fifth century B.C. when trainer Dromeus of Stymphalus won long-distance races in 456 and 460 with significant amounts of meat in his diet. It was also popular among wrestlers, since it added muscle mass and there was no division into weight classes, so the heaviest was the best. However, even in the fifth century B.C., Hippocrates denounced large amounts of meat as an extreme diet which would produce a strange and unstable condition of the body. A Harvard doctor says this about large meat consumption by athletes, "Good red meat works no more magic than the ground lions' teeth with which ancient warriors spiced their meals.'' The myth, however, continues, fueled by reports that Olympic athletes ate large quantities of steak, as many as three at a time. However, figures show that fresh fruit was consumed as frequently as steak, and many of the athletes ate their steaks after their competition, enjoying an unusual luxury.

Having dispelled the myth that a juicy steak is a necessity for anyone with an athletic bent, remember that protein must be taken in sufficient quantities to keep the body going. Most joggers, particularly those with heart conditions, should vary their sources of protein, avoiding high-fat foods and concentrating on low-calorie, low-fat sources of protein.

The main sources of protein are cheese, milk, meat, eggs, grains and legumes. Cheese and eggs are high-fat sources, but should be consumed in small amounts each week. Skim milk cheese should be substituted for creamed cheeses.

Red meat can be included in the diet, but is not necessary. When it is eaten, avoid large portions. A three-ounce steak provides sufficient protein for a meal; a hefty one-pound steak might look good but it is chock full of unnecessary protein as well as harmful saturated fats. Fish and chicken are generally good sources of animal protein. Both are lower in calories than red meat and usually contain fewer saturated fats, although there are some fish that are exceptions. For those who don't want to become vegetarians, fish and chicken should play a large part in the diet.

A vegetarian diet can provide sufficient protein for most people. Pregnant women must be very careful, and it should not be used for children under the age of 20 because their protein need is greater while they are growing. However, a knowledgeable person can combine grains, legumes and nuts with other nutrients to fill his protein requirements.

Fats

Fats have become the villains of the 1970s. Few people aren't aware of the fact that saturated fat is linked to cholesterol, which is probably linked in turn to heart disease. However, there are two kinds of fat, animal and vegetable, and judicious use of them can lessen the problems.

Animal fats tend to come in solid form and are highly saturated. When possible they should be avoided, since they add nothing nutritionally that unsaturated fats don't provide. Vegetable fats, in the form of oil, are generally unsaturated, but the consumer must beware. Palm oil and coconut oil are highly saturated fats and are frequently found in junk food like popcorn, chips and cheesies, which joggers should strike from their diets.

There are also ways to lessen consumption of fats already in food. Skim milk should be substituted for whole milk and cream. Yogurt can be used instead of sour cream. For most fatty foods there are acceptable substitutes which have similar tastes. For the rest of the very rich foods — skip them or your jogging will suffer along with your waistline.

When to Eat and Run

It generally makes good sense not to exercise strenuously right after eating. The reason for this is that, after you eat, the blood is centered in your stomach aiding digestion, and is not as readily available to provide oxygen to the rest of your muscular system.

It's not advisable, then, to imitate Cuban runner Felix Carvajal. A mailman by trade, he started running a marathon in full uniform, including his bulky boots. The day was oppressively hot, so Carvajal started taking his clothes off along the way. To restore his strength, he ate peaches and apples from the trees he passed along the route. Running on a full stomach, he at one point suffered severe stomach pains and had to lie down beside the road for a short while. He eventually got up, however, and finished the race in fourth place—in his underwear.

The break between a meal and exercise can be brief, and once you feel you're ready to hit the track, go ahead. Running before breakfast in the morning is okay too, if you're sure that your body has enough fuel to make it. Whatever you do, though, make sure you don't skip any meals, especially breakfast. It is an easy habit to get into—get up, jog, go to work. Or jog through lunch hour and not have time to eat. The body, however, needs food to replace what was used up. Studies show that runners who eat three meals a day have longer endurance and faster times than those who eat twice a day.

It is not necessary to start the day with a breakfast like track star Cheryl Toussaint. She eats two scrambled eggs, bacon or steak, or any meat leftovers, toast, vanilla malted, with or without an egg, a multivitamin with iron and a cod liver oil capsule. Few joggers would be able to burn up that much food with a jog around the park. However, a healthy breakfast, one which contains carbohydrates, fats and proteins, is a must.

For a jogger with a balanced diet, vitamin supplements shouldn't be necessary. Unless there is a specific deficiency in the diet, supplements may actually harm the runner by causing a vitamin overdose or creating a dependency. If you feel tired, make sure you are eating enough, but don't automatically pop a pill.

In any case, don't skip meals. You won't be doing yourself a favor if you end up giving up jogging because of lack of energy. Remember one of the prime reasons for taking up jogging is to improve the functioning of the cardiovascular system. Pursuing a diet that is balanced nutritionally complements that laudable goal while at the same time helping in the struggle to shed pounds.

Dos and Don'ts

*If you're drinking, don't jog.
*One non-smoker's jog = three smoker's jogs.
*Eat a sensible balance of carbohydrates, fats, and proteins; steer clear of fad diets.
*Make breakfast the day's essential meal.

10

It's Never Too Late — or Too Early

*Senior citizens jog. So do little kids.
Chronological age doesn't matter. Neither
does physical, mental or psychological age
if you're determined to shape up the
jogging way.*

Item: Robert Earle Jones ran
in the annual New York City Marathon in late October 1976. He
finished the 26-mile race. Mr. Jones is the father of the actor,
James Earl Jones. At the time of the marathon, he was 71 years
old. Jerry Pierce finished the course, too. Jerry's from Muncie,
Indiana, and he was ten years old that October.

Item: Torben Ulrich of Denmark had this to say in the
autumn of 1976: "Running is so cleansing. A lot of dirt leaves
your system, a lot of garbage goes." That year Ulrich was a star
on the Grand Masters (over 45) tennis circuit, and he was
running 50 to 75 miles per week. His age? Forty-eight. He also

said, "The whole approach to growing older in athletics is changing. The old generation today grew old without being aware of athletics for them. My generation is just becoming aware. But look ahead 20 to 40 years. People who grow old playing will stay in athletics. We know more of stamina, speed, care of injuries, training, over-training, flexibility, vitamins."

Item: Paul Spangler of San Luis Obispo, California, discovered jogging in 1967. Eight years later, in 1975, he entered the one-mile, two-mile and three-mile events in a track meet. He won the mile race and set a world record for men of his age. At the time, Paul Spangler was 76 years old.

The message rings clear: when it comes to jogging, you're neither too young nor too old. True enough, there's been a minimum of scientific investigation into the pluses and minuses of running for pre-adolescent tads and toddlers, but the kids who have gone in for jogging — the Chuns of Honolulu, for example, six youngsters who are tiny wizards of the marathon — appear to have benefited. And it's clear, too, that for most people, deterioration in fitness begins to set in during those years after the active fun and games of childhood and adolescence have receded into the carefree past. "The dangerous years are between 20 and 30," fitness pioneer Lloyd Percival has pointed out, because they are the years when "young men and women get caught up in their careers and marriages and lose all motivation and opportunity to carry on with sports."

For many people in the 1970s, rescue from the onset of physical sloth is only coming with old age. Instead of accepting deterioration, many senior citizens are rediscovering — or discovering for the first time — the vitality of fitness through jogging. "Running," says Paul Spangler, who wasn't an athlete in his younger years, "has given me an entirely new outlook on life. I have a zest for living I didn't have before. I don't have backaches any more. No colds. I never used to go to bed without a handful of antacid tablets. Now I take none. I know I'm an old bastard, but I don't feel old. I feel young."

Spangler isn't alone. Thousands of men and women over 50, over 60, over 70 and even, in the remarkable cases of Duncan MacLean and Charles Speechley (more about them later), over

80 have reached out to running and jogging as life-savers. If there's a problem with jogging for senior citizens, it's probably that not enough of them can be persuaded to take it up. Of course jogging in later years requires attention to pacing, checking the heart, observing cautions and regulating jogging schedules. Once launched on a sensible program, however, the old folks reap the benefits.

Is Jogging Safe in Later Years?

One lesson that we earthbound mortals have picked up from the space flights of American astronauts and Russian cosmonauts is that the human body and its internal systems deteriorate with lack of use. This decline has become universal in our time mostly through the spread of labor-saving devices and increased leisure time spent in idleness. Spared the toil of our grandparents, we drift gently into physical decline. Unused muscles grow flabby. Hearts falter. Blood flows sluggishly.

That's the grim picture of man's later years. Now for the obvious question: does advanced age make it impossible for senior citizens to turn safely to exercise? Will their hearts, already weakened through indolence, fold under the strain? Is it, in short, too late for the old folks?

Here are some remarks that go to the core of the matter, delivered by Dr. Theodore Klumpp, an American heart specialist and consultant to the President's Council on Physical Fitness and Sports, during a speech in 1974 at the University of North Carolina. "Based on loss of motivation and interest, and to a large extent because of the fear psychosis against exercise and exertion, our middle-aged and older people reduce their physical activities still further with what I believe is especially damaging, if not disastrous, results." The doctor goes on to say, "Atrophy of disuse accentuates the lessened capacity of older persons to react to stress. I have no doubt that such avoidable atrophy is a contributing factor in the death of older persons subjected to accidents, shock, operations, deprivation, stress and prolonged illnesses. Like potent medicines, the proper dosage of stress is beneficial and even life-saving; too much is poison. I look upon moderate or graded stress as necessary to the maintenance of good health, vitality and an adequate reserve against the extremes of stress that in one way or another befall us all. Functional capacities of all systems of the body can only be augmented through moderate stress. From this point of view, exercise may be regarded as the most beneficial form of graded stress.''

The answer to the basic question — is jogging dangerous in the later years? — seems clear. Provided a man or woman is suffering from no serious heart or circulatory damage — aortic valve disease, heart valve problems, the sort of trouble a thorough medical test of cardiopulmonary function and general motor fitness would uncover — then a jogging program is not only safe but it may even prolong and enhance life.

Or, as Paul Spangler answered when he was asked about doctors who warn older patients that running may be harmful, ''That's horse manure — if you do your running sensibly. Doctors are ordinarily too busy curing people to worry about the prevention of disease. An exercise program would be especially good for doctors. They'd live longer and work more efficiently.''

Does Paul Spangler know what he's talking about? He ought to — he's a jogger, and before he retired he was Dr. Spangler, chief surgeon of the US Naval Hospital in Pearl Harbor and later chief surgeon for the California state prison at San Luis Obispo.

Motivation for Older Joggers

For some, it's a basic human emotion that provides the incentive.

''Fear,'' Paul Spangler answers when he's asked how he began jogging. ''Fear of coronary heart disease. In my mid-60s, I saw my friends and colleagues dying all around me. So, instead of lunch, I started jogging.''

But fear, perhaps surprisingly, doesn't work often enough. In the case of many seniors, timidity or resignation to the fates or a perverse sense of dignity makes them shy away from all exercise, including jogging. Too bad, say many geriatric specialists who are coming around to the value of exercise for older people, too bad that the over-60s aren't cottoning on to three basic reasons, apart from physical fitness, for undertaking a jogging program:

1. **Companionship:** "Sweden is the country in which old-age pensioners enjoy the best material conditions," says Beritt Bratlnas Stanton, sports attache for the Swedish Consulate General in the United States. "It is also the country in which they experience the greatest solitude." Increasingly in the 1970s, Sweden has attacked this sad problem with a secret weapon: exercise. "Jogging," Stanton says, "or any other exercise program breaks the pensioners' isolation and gives them more contact with others." The horror of lonely old age isn't confined to Sweden. Nor, to be sure, is the solution that group jogging offers.

2. **Pride:** "One reason I started running," says William Andberg, a sexagenarian marathoner from Minnesota, "was that I became a grandfather. I thought about the grandfather image on TV, the old guy with the gimpy leg. That didn't seem to be me." The physical benefits of jogging — stamina, more supple limbs, clear lungs — pay off in fresh pride and confidence. "People who come to the joys of physical activity late in life," says George Leonard, a runner in his 50s, "emerge all fresh and starry-eyed and virginal."

3. **Mental Health:** Sharper thinking accompanies renewed health and increased confidence. "From observation of my own patients," a Detroit geriatric specialist says, "those three inevitably go together. Men and women who had given up on life from all visible signs, who have grown dull and uninteresting, find the impetus for new intellectual spurts in physical activity."

How to Start Jogging (Senior Division)

The rules for the over-60 crowd are almost the same as for the under-30s. The differences mostly involve matters of degree, bearing in mind the following hints:

1. Don't jog alone. Start with a friend of approximately equal vintage and physical condition. The friend is along for company, for mutual support and for aid in the event of an emergency. Emergencies can be avoided if the jogger makes the very first step in his jogging program a physical checkup.

2. Start by walking. Talk with the companion during the walk. Gradually increase the walking pace. If talking becomes difficult, slow down. If, on the other hand, a walker has enough wind for talking, he has enough for walking and eventually for jogging.

3. Never mind keeping track of distances covered. Just continue moving for 25 minutes to a half-hour. Do it three or four times per week.

4. Don't rush. Actually, such advice is superfluous to most older joggers. "I found," says Walter Jeffries, a Scottish jogger in his early 60s, "that I didn't expect progress in my health to come quickly. Younger men at the club where I often use the track seem to expect instant health. But I knew from the beginning that jogging wouldn't bring overnight results. Other runners of my age feel the same way. We're old enough to have learned patience." Thus, for the senior fellow new to the game, as the sense of effort fades, as distances increase, as times spent on the track or road lengthen—all of which will inevitably occur in a conscientiously followed program — he will progress from walker to jogger, maybe even to runner.

5. "Enjoy yourself." That's the familiar final piece of advice from George Leonard who's enjoying himself.

The Masters

It was David Pain's brainstorm. He's a lawyer in San Diego, California, and an ardent runner. He decided that he'd like to throw a little competitive juice into running for folks his age, the over-40s. In 1968, he organized the first US Masters Track and Field Meet. The notion caught on, older men and women in a variety of age categories fighting it out in all the traditional events from the 100-meter dash through the javelin throw to the distance runs. The first World Master competition took place in Toronto in the summer of 1975 with a grand total of 1,400 competitors flocking from every continent.

The Masters, clearly, is not an event that every jogger should aim for. The primary point of exercise, after all, is sound health, not rugged competition. Still, the Masters participants provide special incentive for older joggers. They've chalked up some amazing feats in the course of their competitions. Monty Montgomery of Sherman Oaks, California, ran a 2:53:03 marathon when he was 65 years old. Erik Ostbye of Sweden, a stripling of 50 did it in 2:28:43. Paul Spangler covers six miles in 45 minutes. But the highest honor goes to "The Tartan Flash." He's Duncan MacLean of Scotland who took on his arch-rival Charles Speechley of England, in the 100-meter dash for their age class at the Masters competition in Toronto. MacLean edged out Speechley, 22.5 seconds to 23.3. MacLean was 90. Speechley was 89.

Jogging for Juniors

The conventional wisdom used to be that kids got enough exercise in natural free-form games that called for plenty of running in the great outdoors. But that idea dates from the pre-TV age, before teeny-boppers and the mini-generation began devoting a few hours per day to Bugs Bunny and reruns of "The Brady Bunch." Television changed the rules, and now such relatively organized activities as jogging may be making sense for non-athletic youngsters who are coming up to adolescence.

Indeed, a kid ought to get his life of exercise launched when he's still in the cradle. That's the view of Allan Scott, a fitness expert from Toronto. "The exercising habit," he says, "should start in infancy. A baby should be allowed the freedom to kick and stretch its body." From then on, according to Scott, wise parents will encourage their growing toddlers to involve themselves in all forms of physical activity, from primitive to sophisticated. "As you plan and set aside time for your children's studies and lessons," he counsels, "so too should you set aside time for a family exercise program."

It makes sense. Jogging for youngsters, as a choice of exercise, isn't going to do any harm, provided they've passed the usual checkup from the pediatrician, and it's bound to tone up their physiques. What's more, there's some evidence that running can offer a child benefits of the mind and spirit. Dr. Thaddeus Kostrubala, the San Diego psychiatrist, has chronicled some successes that jogging has brought to his younger patients. One of them, a ten-year-old hyperactive boy, was following a familiar pattern at school: trouble-maker, poor student, unpopular with teachers and students. Dr. Kostrubula, after a shot at medication, prescribed running. The boy tried it, like it, stayed at it. The ultimate result? Goodbye medication and hyperactivity. Hello, good grades.

Such tales have an evangelical ring to them, but it seems to be true that an improved performance in school often goes hand in hand with a regular regimen of running. Both activities, studying and running, demand discipline and concentration, and champions of jogging for kids claim that physical and mental activities complement each other. A sound mind in a sound body. Maybe so, but the priorities for young runners have probably been best expressed by a cardiologist from Honolulu named Dr. Hing Hua Chun. He's a runner and father of six running children. The kids, ranging from pre-teens to mid-teens, have run marathons and established age-group distance records through the 1970s. All six, perhaps more to the point, have also scored as honor students at their various schools. And it's with the children's scholastic achievments in mind that Dr. Hing Hua Chun once summed up his approach to the family's running:

"I hope the kids will run competitively as long as they enjoy it, but track isn't a career sport. Running has helped us build a lasting base of endurance in case we need it, but scholarship will provide a choice of careers. Even if the kids abandon running, the expanded cardiovascular system we've implanted can be reactivated quickly if they should wish to resume in later life."

Do's and Don'ts

*A senior jogger's first stop is at his doctor's office for a complete medical checkup.

*Jog for pride, jog for companionship, jog for sharper mental, processes.

*Exercise can't begin too early when the goal is lifelong fitness.

Not For Men Only

*Women aren't immune to heart problems —
or other disasters that low-grade
fitness can visit on men. Jogging may be the
answer — but jogging with a few differences.*

Dr. Kenneth Cooper thinks
that women rather than men are the principal victims of the
sedentary age. "The only walking many women get in," he
says, "is in parking lots." A study carried out in 1974 among
1,234 Canadian men and women by the federal Health and
Welfare Department concluded that the least fit category of
citizens were women between the ages of 20 and 29, the prime
child-bearing years. A New York exercise physiologist points
out that the jobs many younger women do, such as secretarial,
clerical and light assembly-line work, are conducive to all sorts
of physical complaints. "Neck pains, back aches, the plain old

112

secretary's spread in the rear end — too many women catch them," the physiologist says. "Women in routine jobs are particular victims, but so are housewives, since all the modern labor-saving devices around the home have made them less active during the day. The real complaint that all these women share is lousy physical condition." Women whose occupations and professions take them into what used to be called "the men's world," are also beginning to suffer from "the men's ailments." So far, women have been far less susceptible to heart problems than men. Estrogen, the exclusively female hormone, has acted as a natural immunizing agent against cardiac troubles, at least in the years before menopause. But the rise of feminism, bringing more women to positions of responsibility, and exposing them increasingly to stress situations, has also brought a rising incidence of coronary disease in women.

The Myths That Keep Women Indoors

It's true enough that, for the most part, women possess a smaller proportion of muscle to fatty tissue than men, that women's heart size measures to about 85 to 90 percent of men's heart size, that women have a smaller oxygen-intake and oxygen-carrying capacity than men, that women's bones, muscles, tendons and ligaments are more delicate than men's. But there are two responses that women can offer to such documented data. One is to ponder whether such differences are truly biological or whether, at the root of things, they're the result of women's social conditioning. And the second response is to mutter a disgusted "So what?"

"The hardest step for a woman who wants to run is the first one out the door," says Joan Ullyot, a San Francisco physician who discovered jogging in 1970 when she was 29 and has since entered and won long-distance races. "It's the hardest because that's where she has to lay aside all her old ways of thinking."

Until recently society has conditioned women to concentrate on the gentle graces and to leave to men the activities that call for hearty effort and perspiration. Little girls were taught that boys won't like them if they go in for too much rough-house stuff, and at public and high schools a tiny fraction of the funds allotted to male athletics was made available to girls who preferred a more active role than cheerleading for the boys' teams. Throughout their education, little emphasis was placed on female fitness. Happily this situation is rapidly changing, as both men and women recognize the benefits of physical conditioning. "If no other women were running in it," Kathy Switzer has written of her feat in cracking the sex barrier at the Boston Marathon in 1967, "it was only because they hadn't yet discovered what fun long-distance running can be."

Exactly. And such an attitude should apply to every woman from the shy, beginning jogger to the ambitious marathoner. It's all a matter, in a sense, of cracking the conspiracy, of tossing off the customs and training that have worked to confine women to the kitchen and parlor and to keep them out of the fresh air.

Is there any physical reason for women to shy away from jogging and running? Is there any substance to the myths that have kept women indoors? Kenneth Cooper provides the best answer: "A heart is a heart, lungs are lungs, blood vessels are blood vessels. They have no sex and the effect on all is the same."

Or, as Arthur Lydiard, the pioneering New Zealand trainer, put it as early as 1960, "Women can train as long as men can train, can run as far as men can run, like men they can do it seven days a week all year through. A few years ago, people would have considered this either impossible or unwise."

Women, in short, have nothing to lose but a few shopworn myths.

Small Cautions

Based on his field testing, Dr. Kenneth Cooper believes that women joggers and runners don't need to try as hard. Because their hearts and lung capacities are smaller, Cooper thinks, because their aerobic capacity is less, women can become fit by taking on a program that is slightly scaled down from the men's program. Thus, in Cooper's prescriptions, fully documented in *Aerobics For Women*, co-authored by Cooper and his wife Millie, he permits women joggers, walkers and runners to win points by covering shorter distances than men and to aim for fewer points per week than men. He doesn't discourage women from aiming higher, but at the same time he doesn't insist they meet the standards he set for men.

Cooper's philosophy does not contradict his own and Lydiard's and other experts' exhortations that hearts and muscles are sexless and that women can keep pace with men in the drive to fitness. There may come a day when women runners will equal or pass men runners in world-record times; indeed, Dr. Ernst van Aaken, the German coach and physiologist, believes that women's metabolism is better suited than men's for endurance and that women will eventually outperform men in the marathon. "Women," van Aaken says, "run off their fat." But until then, the majority of women runners and joggers should make allowance for their centuries of socio-biological conditioning.

Caution number one: Don't attempt to match strides or fitness or programs or amibition with husband, father, brother or boy friend. Proceed, after the usual medical checkup and fitness evaluation, on a personal basis.

Caution number two, especially intended for beginners: Take it easy. "The trouble with almost all women who come in here," says the female manager of a health club and indoor track in a Chicago suburb, "is that they've forgotten how to run." Distressingly typical. Many women stopped running on the day they played their last game of British Bulldog or Hide-and-Go-Seek. Their running muscles have gone slack, and, as the Chicago observer points out, "Those women lose in two ways — they get more muscle pains than men, mostly because they start off in too much of a rush, and they get discouraged more easily." Her answer? "Women should be very careful about warming up before they run or jog, and they shouldn't get too ambitious right off the bat."

Jogging and the Female Form

There are obvious anatomical differences between men and women, and women have to make certain adjustments for them in their equipment and their jogging routines.

Breasts: "Unfortunately, many women get into fitness in the belief that they'll acquire larger busts," says a women exercise physiologist in Miami, "and some commercial fitness organizations take advantage of this belief. What the instructors do in these clubs is give the women exercises that build up their back muscles. When the women measure their busts, they may appear to be bigger, but that isn't due to any increase in actual breast size. One thing that proper exercise can do is increase the size of the muscles that underlie the breasts, the pectoralis major and minor, and that may have the effect of making the bust larger."

That takes care of the fraud. Now for the facts:

1. No one is absolutely certain whether jogging reduces or enlarges breast size. Women have reported both results. What is certain is that jogging adds tone and firmness to all tissue and muscle, and that includes the tissue in the breasts and the pectoral muscles that support them.

2. A brassiere is a necessity for women joggers, both for comfort and for back-up to the breast-supporting ligaments. A bra also helps jogging style, as a Los Angeles physician has pointed out. "Especially for a heavy-breasted woman, the lack of support that a brassiere normally ensures could throw a jogger rather badly off balance."

Legs and Figure: "Since I started running," says Joan Ullyot, the California physician, "I've gone from a size fourteen to a size ten."

Running, to be sure, can never be solely responsible for a slimming effect, and exercise physiologists emphasize that, without care in eating habits and perhaps adjustments in diet, no woman can expect to drop large amounts of unwanted weight through jogging alone. Still, jogging promotes a trimmer figure in several ways. It burns calories. It firms muscles in the thighs and other parts of the body. It replaces fat with muscle. And it generally encourages slimness in body areas where women prefer slimness, the hips for example. Jogging can also help to avoid or reduce blotchy varicose veins simply by strengthening the muscles and veins in the legs where the unsightly marks are likely to occur.

Jogging and the Menstrual Cycle

At the 1964 Olympic Games in Tokyo, doctors selected 75 women competitors for study. In the course of the two weeks of competition, the women under examination were in all stages of the menstrual cycle. Results of the study? Menstruation appeared to have no impact on the standings in races. Some women at the beginning of their cycles won gold medals.

The principle revealed in Tokyo by and large applies to woman joggers. If menstruation is regarded as another form of stress, then a woman who has conditioned her body by jogging will be better equipped to withstand menstruation's physical and emotional strains. Jogging contributes to more efficient blood circulation and more powerful muscular strength, two formidable weapons in resisting cramps and fatigue.

"Reasonable physical exercise during menstruation is not merely allowed," writes Millie Cooper, "it's often helpful, especially to women who have painful menstrual periods."

Jogging and Pregnancy

For a young—or maybe not-so-young—married woman who is planning a family, jogging qualifies as a sensible preparation for motherhood. "The toning that exercises such as jogging give to the muscles of the back and the abdomen," according to one family health report compiled by the US Drug and Health Administation, "contributes to a much less painful delivery of the baby. It also accelerates a return of the mother's stomach to its original firm and healthy state."

As for jogging during pregnancy, a woman is advised by most exercise physiologists to obtain initial approval from her obstetrician. If that step is safely passed, then a pregnant woman may jog to her heart's content up to the sixth month. She may even initiate a jogging program during the first six months of pregnancy. For the last three months, however, nothing more than a good brisk walk is advised. Those six months of jogging can prove invaluable in easing such afflictions as cramps, constipation and other discomforts associated with pregnancy.

Jogging and the Menopause

Hot flashes, fatigue and depression are all symptoms that result from the reduced output of estrogen during menopause. Jogging will hardly eliminate these problems, but its physical and psychological benefits can at least lessen their toll for the menopausal woman, bringing increased confidence in her physical appearance just at a time when she feels she may be losing her femininity.

"The first line of defense in the menopause," says a New York physician who specializes in ailments most common to women, "is a healthy body. I've operated on many middle-aged women, and it happens without fail that the ones who make the quickest recovery are the ones who've paid attention to their bodies, the exercise nuts, the tennis freaks, the joggers."

All of which seems to make it unanimous—for middle-aged and older women, for pregnant women, for women keen on a fit body, jogging holds some answers. As recently as the mid-1960s, jogging for women wasn't considered seemly. But in a more liberated time, when fitness isn't confined to a brave and select minority of women, jogging is rightfully assuming its important role in the daily lives of more and more women.

Dos and Don'ts

*Women joggers reap the same fitness benefits as men.
*Jogging can ease many of the discomforts of menstruation, menopause, and early pregnancy .
*Don't try to match strides with the male joggers in your life.

12

Sex and Other Games

Want to upgrade your tennis game?
Improve your squash and golf?
Looking to regenerate your performance on that
ultimate field of athletics — the bed?
Jogging can help.

T he Swedish women athletes, on a competitive track-and-field tour of North America in 1971, had a grievance. They talked about it among themselves, wondering and diagnosing and complaining, until ultimately they presented their frustration to one of the Canadian officials in charge of the tour.

"What is wrong with North American men?" the spokeswoman for the group said, searching for the proper delicacy of phrase. "Why do they lack, ah, emotional stamina?"

Put in words of one syllable, North American men were, as far as the Swedish women were concerned, flops in bed. The men ran the course of their sexual repertoires in a swift few minutes. By the time the women were warming up to action, the men were rolling over, fatigued, to grab some rest or to grab their pants. To the well-conditioned Swedish women's dismay, the North Americans had no staying power, no durability, no sexual fitness.

Are joggers better bedmates? Well, they may not necessarily display more sexual imagination than non-joggers, but the evidence is that they're at least in better physical condition to carry out their sexual inclinations, whatever they maybe. Consider the response of Lloyd Percival, for years a most respected diagnostician of fitness, when he was asked for his assessment of a physical-conditioning program on a man or woman's sex life.

"Truthfully," Percival answered, "fitness has a very definite positive influence on sexual vitality, and I think that many people, though they don't always talk about it readily, found this their big incentive towards fitness."

Indeed, the relationship works both ways. The drive to shape up in the sack motivates men and women to get themselves into a jogging fitness program, and a fit body gives them increased sexual vitality. And the same relationship extends into other sporting areas. Want to jazz up your tennis? Better squash? A sharper game of soccer with the mates on Sunday mornings at the local field? Get out and jog ... or, wait a minute, maybe jogging doesn't apply as much to one game — hockey. There are complicating factors, which we'll come to, to take into account when jogging is considered as an aid to hockey and a few other sports. But the basic premise remains constant: jogging, while it brings its own reward of a fitter body, can also yield dividends in more accomplished performances at games like tennis and squash and ... sex.

The Sex Life of the Jogger

Let's begin with a four-year study, completed in the late winter of 1972, in which the Fitness Institute of Toronto administered exhaustive tests to 4,421 men and 1,675 women between the ages of 18 and 70. The study, not surprisingly, arrived at all sorts of conclusions, and in the fascinating area of sex vis-à-vis fitness, it had this to say:

"While women retain an interest in and capability for sex to a much greater age than men, a man's sexual activity depends largely on his physiological age — that is, his degree of fitness rather than his actual years.

"This activity is entirely recoverable through exercise by men between the ages of 35 and 55. There is absolutely no reason why men, as well as women, cannot maintain a vigorous sex life into their 70s."

That should be a plain enough warning to men. But if it isn't, let's consult a Los Angeles psychiatrist who, in an anonymous article published in the fall of 1975, pointed out that the benefits of sound conditioning to a man's sexual performance fall into two categories: mechanical and cosmetic. "If a man thinks he looks good, if he feels that his physical appearance is trim and muscular, then he is bound to perform up to those standards in his lovemaking. At any rate, he's going to go to great lengths to try and meet the standards. It's the self-image that's important, the image of the fit and virile stud, and a man can reach for that image by working out, running, jogging, that sort of solid physical activity."

He goes on to say, "A man must have the physical equipment to follow through. That is, he must have endurance. Sturdy thigh muscles are essential. Firm muscles help in almost every part of the body in effective lovemaking. He must be fit enough not to suffer muscle cramps at crucial moments in bed. And, of course, it's a steady program of exercise that gives our sexual athlete these benefits."

Summing up, the psychiatrist emphasized that "The psychology of feeling good in bed and the physical equipment to carry out the feelings merge into a powerful sexual package."

It's inarguable that the man or woman who looks fit is going to be on the receiving end of more invitations to bed than the overweight slob, and it's an equally sure bet that he or she is going to function longer and more effectively. But there are some cautions to consider.

1. As Lloyd Percival pointed out, the drive to improve one's

sex life is a powerful incentive to get fit . . . maybe *too* powerful. Some over-eager Casanovas, in his experience, rush into fitness programs that overtax their bodies. They end up fatigued with aching limbs, and as for their sex lives, well, they usually lose the girl in the last reel. A few aches and pains won't hold a man back, but completely depleted resources will. Percival's advice: don't let dreams of conquest make you too ambitious.

2. A curious — and potentially heart-breaking — problem arises when one love partner takes up a jogging program that makes him or her fit and raring to go in bed while the other still out of shape is somewhat less enthusiastic. Despair may lie ahead. The situation demands enormous patience from the fit partner. Either that, or it calls for resolution on the part of the sluggard to get himself or herself into a shape-up program. Or there's a third alternative — divorce and separation.

3. The California psychiatrist recommends a modest program of calisthenics to accompany jogging as a conditioner for sexual activity. Situps ("to give the stomach firmness and a clean line"). Pushups ("a woman making love likes to feel strength in her mate's shoulders and upper arms"). A little weight-lifting ("firm back muscles"). But, the psychiatrist emphasizes, the most important single ingredient is "stamina, the durability to perform one's own fantasies and to carry on long enough to satisfy one's partner's fantasies."

One more caution: let's keep in mind *which* partner it is you're supposed to be satisfying. A letter in the spring of 1976 to Ann Landers, the advice columnist, came from a woman whose husband's dedication to jogging struck her as slightly suspect. The hardy fellow would jog off each morning before breakfast no matter what the weather, fierce gales, blinding snowstorms, dripping heat, and jog back an hour later ravenous for breakfast. One fatal morning, in the teeth of a near hurricane, she followed him on his jog, keeping a discreet distance. The husband hurried down the block, ducked up a couple of streets and jogged straight through a front door into the home and arms of a local divorcee. Miss Landers recommended that the complaining wife burn hubby's jogging shoes.

Jogging and Other Sports

Let's set the stage with a couple of quotes.

1. Allan Scott, fitness director: "Fitness isn't the answer to everything for an athlete. A player has to have some talent for the games, too. For a bad player, getting into shape may only mean that he'll be bad longer."

2. Paul Lessack, chief exercise physiologist at the medical school of Rutgers University, New Jersey: "I haven't found any evidence of good cardiovascular endurance in any of the pro athletes I've examined, and that includes most tennis players, football and baseball and hockey players. They get high marks in brute strength and in horsepower, but in fact they are all in very poor shape."

What we're confronted with here is a delicate balance. Suppose you're a tennis hacker and you take up jogging, counting on it as a sure-fire preparation for the thrashing you've always intended to inflict on Bjorn Borg once you lure him on to the tennis court. Now let's suppose, a non-jogger, you're the champ at your local club and Bjorn Borg comes to town. You challenge him, expecting victory. Uh, uh, you lose both ways. According to Allan Scott, fitness isn't going to help you to victory if you haven't talent for the game, and according to Paul Lessack, you need sound cardiovascular fitness as well as a generous dose of talent to overcome the sheer strength and power of a player like Bjorn Borg.

Still, we might as well look on the cheery side and recognize that, no matter how small your store of talent is for any given game, a jogging program is bound to provide the stamina you need to work longer and harder at improving your skills. "The best way to get better at tennis is to play as much as possible," Allan Scott says, "and the only way to stick that out is to develop the endurance for lots of play." There are advantages to jogging, too, other than the skill-improving benefits. For one, good conditioning through running makes you a more popular partner; after all, there's nothing more grating on the nerves than beginning a brisk set of singles only to find it ending 30 minutes later because the pooper on the other side of the net has run out of steam. And fitness will increase your own pleasure in the game. How much more fun it is to run down an opponent's return when it's a shot that in your pre-jogging days you'd have given up on as hopelessly out of your range. Probably the key thought to keep in mind, the basic truth that lies behind all these benefits and pleasures and advantages, is that you don't really play games to get fit. If anything, it works the other way around — you get fit to play games. And that applies to almost any sport you can name.

Golf

"Occasional rigorous exercise," says Paul Lessack, "a weekend game of golf, for example, in the case of a man who spends most of his time physically idle behind a desk, is highly dangerous and maybe fatal."

Golfers, of all part-time athletes, may be the gents who need jogging most of all. The sudden exertions that the game demands — pulling the club back for a long tee shot, blasting behind the ball to lift it out of a bunker, socking into a four-iron to reach the green in two—can send the heart rate zooming up the scale. Dangerous? You better believe it. The obvious answer is to jog and to build up the heart to accommodate such stresses. That's defensive planning. Now let's consider offensive strategy. Murray Tucker, Canadian golf pro, is firm in the view that "many medium-handicap and high-handicap golfers lose strokes on the back nine of their games because they run out of energy and make poor shots. They play below their real abilities when they lose two assets at the same time — strength and concentration."

Enough said. Get jogging.

Squash

Here's something curious. Squash players new to the game had better be solidly fit while veterans with the racquet don't need to measure as high on the fitness scale.

In the case of the latter group, the fellows who've been

knocking a squash ball around for ten or fifteen years, they've mastered the game's strategy and they know how to position themselves for a tricky bounce or a nick off the wall with a minimum of effort and movement. Dr. Terry Kavanagh of the Toronto Rehabilitation Centre tested a friend who'd played championship squash over a couple of decades or more, and discovered that, in overall fitness, the squash demon scored no higher than "the average sedentary male of the same age." Kavanagh's pal moved so few steps over such a small and circumscribed territory on the court that he placed little strain on his cardiovascular system. Thus, the message is clear for superior players: treat squash as a mere diversion and take up jogging to maintain fitness.

As for the newcomer, the process works in reverse. He needs a high degree of fitness to handle a 40-minute game of squash. It's a non-stop sport with almost no pauses for catching breath and regrouping resources. According to Dr. Kenneth Cooper, squash rates just below running, swimming, cycling and walking as an aerobic activity. That's okay for exercise, but we're talking now of skill. If you want to improve your squash game, then it's helpful, probably essential, to jog your way to a good level of fitness before you hit the courts. That, at any rate, is the opinion of one Australian squash pro who points out that "The crunch in any 40-minute squash game comes in the last 15 minutes, which is when you separate the men from the boys, the fit from the unfit. Two men can play equally in terms of skill for half a game or more, but then conditioning shows, or lack of it, when one fellow won't have the reserve to keep chasing the ball, to keep moving into position. He develops feet of lead."

Tennis

Tennis is another stop-and-go sport. It consists of relatively tranquil intervals interrupted by sudden moments of quick, almost savage action intensified by the fierce competitive sense that the game seems to bring out in its players. A jogging progam will help any player prepare for such assaults, gener-

ally by developing endurance and particularly by strengthening the heart and legs. The heart must be in sound pumping
order to withstand the strain of two hours or so of singles. And
the legs need the extra conditioning because tennis exerts
special pressure on leg muscles. Tennis players seldom
straighten their legs. Waiting for a serve or preparing to return
a shot, players crouch. They bend their legs. That's tough and
demands the extra strength and toning that jogging builds. It's
probably useful to practice a special "tennis-leg" exercise.
Take up the crouching stance you'd use while waiting to
return a serve. Spread the legs slightly more widely apart. Sink
slowly until the thighs are parallel to the ground. Hold, gently
bouncing, for 30 seconds. Relax. Build to 60 seconds at a crack,
three sets per time.

Hockey

When Team Canada was preparing to play against the world's
other hockey powers in the Canada Cup tournament of 1976,
Richard Martin was unhappy with the squad's training program. Richard Martin is the high-scoring Buffalo Sabres
winger, and he had this to say about Team Canada's dry-land
conditioning sessions in Montreal's Mount Royal Park: "When
we go up the mountain, we break into two groups—those who
want to run and those who don't. I don't, because I find that
running bothers my leg muscles. You use different muscles
when you skate from the ones you use when you run."

Richard Martin may have a point. On the other hand, he may
unconsciously be supporting a point that Paul Lessack makes,
namely that "Organized sport is still in the Dark Ages when it
comes to training and conditioning." Lessack developed his
thoughts about pro athletes' training in a lengthy interview he
gave in the summer of 1976:

"The typical cardiovascular fitness program in pro sports,"
Lessack said, "is for the team to go out and jog a mile before or
after practice. In fact, based on scientific principles, this is a
poor program. The best program to increase cardiovascular
strength is one which utilizes integral training, a method of

conditioning that integrates work periods with rest periods. This is true for the pro athlete and for the ordinary adult.

"Rather than going out and running a mile as fast as you can until you're totally fatigued, the thing to do is to run a quarter mile and do it at a certain pace, then stop and rest for two minutes and repeat that six or eight times. That way, the pro athlete is doing more work under less fatigue and getting greater cardiovascular benefits."

For the part-time amateur athlete, for the aging jock who likes to get together with the fellas from college hockey days for a little shinny and beer on an early Sunday morning, Lessack says his conditioning program goes double and in spades. Men who are not in shape and lead business lives behind desks and the wheels of cars are asking for trouble if they strap on skates without first preparing their bodies in a fitness program carried out over a long enough period to strengthen the heart against the sudden exertions that the stops, spurts and bumps of hockey bring on. Basketball? Touch football? Soccer? Even softball? Same thing. All place severe burdens on the untrained heart.

Now what about Richard Martin's complaint, that running muscles are different from skating muscles? Denis Potvin, the all-star defenceman for the New York Islanders and a Team Canada teammate of Martin's, had the answer. At first, he agreed with Martin that running might not be all it was cracked up to be as a hockey conditioner. Later, though, as the Canada Cup series progressed, as Potvin turned into one of the bright lights of the series, he admitted that the running program had "built up my stamina." Were his leg muscles confused? "That worked itself out as soon as I'd done a little skating."

Snow Shoveling

Hardly a sport, but a necessary and strenuous activity for most homeowners, snow shoveling can be made easier by following these rules:

1. Jog in place before laying a hand on the shovel. Exertion

lies ahead and the heart muscles must be pumping blood in preparation.

2. Protect the area of the heart with warm clothing. Cold weather constricts the arteries at a time when your body is in most need of a strong supply of blood.

3. If you're over 40, out of shape and physically inactive, hire a kid to shovel the damn stuff.

Dos and Don'ts

*Stamina is the key to success in any sport, especially sex.
*Don't be a strict weekend sportsman. Jog on the days between Sunday and Saturday.
*One-sport athletes don't usually reach more-than-average fitness. They need an extra — jogging.

13

Jog Together — Stay Together?

*Everyone knows about the loneliness
of the long-distance runner. What few
people realize is that he's content in his loneliness.
But other runners and joggers crave a little
company with their exercise. The facts seem
to be that there are important
benefits to both jogging styles.
Alone or in a crowd?*

Let's begin by mulling over a handful of relevant observations.

From Tex Maule in his book, *Running Scarred:* "By the end of the first year, I had run a total of 714 miles and spent 105 hours, 17 minutes, 4.2 seconds on the track, plus probably three times as much time boring people talking about it."

From Tom MacMillan, an officer of Participaction, the non-profit company promoting fitness in Canada: "One of the things about fitness is that it becomes evangelical. People get so excited when they see what it does for them that they want to spread the word."

From Edmund Burke, the great eighteenth-century English politician-philosopher, speaking from the stump a few days before the national election of 1780: "Applaud us when we run. Console us when we fall. Cheer us when we recover. But let us pass on — for God's sake, let us pass on!"

No sense in shrinking from the hard truth: the fact is that the jogger can on occasion display the traits of two of society's less appealing types, the club bore and the spoiled brat. And coping with these sides of the jogger's personality presents a demanding chore for wives, husbands, parents, children and associates of the runner. Listening to an enthusiastic runner who's just handled five miles in under 35 minutes and wants to detail every yard of the run can be trying. Be patient, you say? Ah yes, but suppose it's the third time in a week that you've endured the step-by-step account? Not even Job could summon such patience.

There are two answers to the dilemma: join the jogger or, as Edmund Burke might be construed as counseling, applaud him. The pat on the back is especially necessary to the beginning jogger. He is, after all, launched on a bold new experiment, one calculated to rescue his health, and if the going turns rugged in the early months, as it inevitably does, then he needs rallying support from all those with a stake, moral or financial or familial, in his new life. A little cheering from the sidelines will help nudge him toward his jogging objective. Indeed it might conceivably make the difference between persevering at his program or, in a moment of unsupported discouragement, chucking it in favor of longer mornings in bed and open-ended evenings in front of the TV set.

The other alternative, joining the jogger if you can't silence him, can bring rewards for all concerned. It not only converts the wife, husband or old buddy who previously functioned mainly as a sounding board into a potential fitness nut, but it also may give the original jogger a new lease on his running program. Henceforth he'll no longer notch up the miles on his own. He'll have company. And that may make a significant difference in his jogging life.

Group Jogging vs. Solo Flights

The notion of jogging *en famille* or with a pal or two introduces the much broader, more fundamental question: is it better to jog in a crowd or to take a solitary canter? Maybe it boils down to a matter of personality. Dr. Kenneth Cooper is categorical in his view that "The typical American hates doing anything alone, and he'll do things in a group, especially exercise, that he wouldn't think of doing alone." Ergo, argues the good doctor, "activity breeds competition and competition breeds activity." Bill Bowerman partly disagrees. "Jogging is *never* competitive," he thinks. "Most important," he continues, "be content to jog at your own pace." Once the competitive element is eliminated, however, Bowerman goes along with Dr. Cooper in favoring group runs. "Jogging is good family fun," he believes. "Get the whole group on a regular schedule and jog together."

On the other hand, there's the gut feeling of Gary Ross, the Canadian novelist who runs—or perhaps he's the runner who writes. He put his view in a 1976 letter from the village in Yorkshire where he spent most of a year scribbling and jogging. "I met a bunch of guys who are collectively the Harrogate Track Club. I briefly entertained the notion of ceding my mobile existence to said track club's existence; then rebelled. I run to cleanse my mind, my lungs and my cloudy impressions of the planet Erf, as we say in Yorkshire, not to synchronise footsteps with guys who assist in the production of McIntosh candy bars."

Maybe it's a matter of personality, but maybe, too, it's valuable to add up the merits of both styles, group running and solo jogging. Let's look first at the advantages of the group approach.

Overcomes self-consciousness: The beginning jogger is almost bound to feel certain reservations, to put the situation mildly, when he steps out the front door in his spanking new sweat suit and prances for the first time past neighbors who, he's certain, are snickering behind their curtains. For that beginner, a crowd is probably the answer: if he's convinced he looks crazy in his jogging role, how much easier it is to bear in the company of other crazies.

Combats the jeers: When Frank Shorter, the great American marathoner, was training in New Mexico in the late 1960s, his father was often compelled to accompany him by car, riding shotgun, to ward off kids in jalopies who threated Shorter with sticks, stones, beer bottles and other implements of war. The situation is hardly that serious in most civilized communities. Still, much of the world remains populated with smart apples who get their kicks from hurling jeers or worse at solitary joggers. Such characters are rarely so brave when they're confronted by joggers in a mass.

Provides competition: For those joggers who confirm Dr. Cooper's opinion that competition breeds activity, the company of fellow joggers might create the needed stimulus to stick to a fitness program. To most joggers, a little competition goes a long way, but to the hardy few, it may be a necessity.

Offers company: There's a summer camp for kids in upper New York State called Camp Na-Sho-Pa. It has a jogging program which is designed, so the folks at Na-Sho-Pa claim, "to combine physical fitness, achievement of goals and friendship." Exactly. Jogging in a group *is* a friendly activity, and for those with a gregarious bend to their personality, matching strides with four or five like-minded souls on an early morning run offers one of life's joys.

So much for group jogging. Now consider the advantages of the solo run.

Allows jogger to set own pace: There's nothing more frustrating and potentially defeating for a jogger than to find himself in company that's too fast or too slow. A jogger must search out his own rhythm — fleet and erratic, leisurely and dogged, somewhere in between — and the optimum circumstances for discovering it arise when one runs to the beat of one's own drummer.

Carves out thinking time: Some men and women arrive at their most creative ideas in mid-jog. Others cook up their most luscious fantasies during a long run. But how can anybody think or fantasize when a couple of other joggers are huffing, gasping, panting and gabbing into each ear?

Stimulates and exhilarates: Running alone can induce a sort of magic. Let Gary Ross express it: "Running for me is commu-

nion with self, totally solitary as opposed to social, and thus
spiritual to the nth degree.''

Alone or in a group? Take your pick.

The Family that Jogs Together

A feature film called *Second Wind* showed up in first-run
North American movie houses in the summer of 1976 with a
scary message for joggers. *Second Wind* told the story of a
young stockbroker who takes up jogging to keep himself in
good trim. He jogs, he runs, and he gets hooked. He grows so
obsessed with running that he lets his stockbroking slide,
ignores his wife, and even turns aside a pass from a glamor
puss at the office. His life turns topsy turvy in his sudden and
shocking new drive to accomplish astounding feats of running. Jogging converts him into a nut case. At the last moment,
however, sound sense triumphs and the young fellow is saved
for wife and business, but *Second Wind* still raises a nervous
question: can jogging destroy a happy family?

Dr. George Sheehan doesn't think so. He's the New Jersey
cardiologist and jogging prophet, and he says that "running
can rebuild families." Dr. Sheehan's point is that the simple
act of jogging together can rejuvenate family contacts that
have withered over too many desultory dinner conversations
and too many silent hours in the television room. The family
that jogs together, he's saying, is apt to stay together.

Well, it's a cozy theory, but does it translate into reality?
Probably so. At least, there's enough evidence to suggest that
Dr. Sheehan may be on to something solid. Take the Pamakids
Club in San Francisco. The name, as you've no doubt already
sorted out, stands for pa, ma and kids, and the club, with
dozens of families enrolled, is successfully dedicated to family
running. Or there are Joe and Adele Bradley of Toronto, a
middle-aged couple who got into jogging in the 1970s when
their daughter Sue won a spot as a track competitor on Canada's 1976 Olympic team. "When we saw how much Sue was
prepared to sacrifice to train," Joe explains, "we felt the least

we could do was to make some effort ourselves." Or turn to the Epstein family of Brooklyn. Irving and Marion are both crowding 60, but they maintain the long family tradition of jogging with son Ed and daughter Laraine, who got so accomplished in runs with mother and dad that she graduated to the Boston Marathon. "Perhaps it's selfish or sentimental," Irving Epstein says, "but mama and I want to run with our children."

So, apparently, do plenty of other mums and dads. But there are, according to jogging wise men who've looked at the matter, a few cautionary measures that togetherness enthusiasts ought to observe.

1. "It's easier to teach your wife or kid to jog than it is to drive," says Harrison Andover, a Chicago psychologist who jogs a couple of miles a day with his family, "but it takes some of the same patience. Not everybody starts out with an equal degree of fitness, especially if one member of the family has been into jogging for a year or more before the others, and the ones who are capable of more speed and more distance have to rein themselves in at the beginning. Otherwise, the jogging path may be a route to the divorce court."

2. *Runner's World* magazine hit on a nice point in its May 1973 issue when it discussed "the healthy paradox in family running. The group shares the experience while running as individuals. They're in it together, yet they're on their own ... Each one has to do his own work. He can't shove it onto daddy or brother." Jogging with the family, in other words, imposes a heavier burden in terms of measuring up than does jogging alone. Be warned.

3. Family running also calls for family responsibility. "Once you're committed to jogging with your family," says Harrison Andover, "then you've got to stick to the schedule that the unit sets up. If everybody's decided on three or four or five morning jogs per week or whatever, then you've got to show up for three or four or five morning jogs per week or whatever. Otherwise you're not providing the support that the other members of the family have legitimately come to expect."

Once these rules are agreed to, then any jogging family ought to arrive at the bliss that John Butterfield, a jogging devotee with a wife and three children, wrote of in his booklet

Beginning Running: "I could go on and on about running and the joys it has brought us individually and collectively. As a family, we have something we can share and that we enjoy sharing."

On the Sidelines

Dr. Bruce Ogilvie, a psychologist at San Jose State University, helped launch the Institute for the Study of Athletic Motivation in the late 1960s, and his Institute's think tank arrived at this unhappy conclusion. "It's the wife or girl friend in the life of the runner who often has to suffer. A man who loves to run has to have a very special wife or girl friend to understand and accept his running, which may be a competitor to her."

There are a couple of sidelights to Dr. Ogilvie's sad news. One is that his warning zeros in principally on the serious marathon runner, not the mile-a-day jogger; and the other is that, with all the women electing for jogging in the 1970s, it may equally be the husband or the boy friend who must demonstrate heroic patience. In any event, Dr. Ogilvie's point is well taken. In jogging, as in war, they also serve who only stand and wait.

Dr. Terence Kavanagh is sufficiently concerned about the problem of the people on the sidelines that he holds regular gatherings to explain to wives and girl friends exactly what their men are up to in their long hours on the jogging track. The purpose of the gatherings is simply, says Kavanagh, "to help these women help their husbands." Most often Kavanagh's low-key explanatory approach works. It did in the case of Mrs. Herman Roberts, wife of the first heart patient ever to be accepted as an offfical entrant in the Boston Marathon (in 1975 Roberts finished in three hours and 20 minutes, placing him in about 1500th place of 2500 entrants). "Certainly Herman's running is time-consuming," Mrs. Roberts says. "In fact, our daughter was two years old before all three of us ever had Sunday dinner together. Herman was always out training. But that's a small price to have him alive and healthy."

Not all wives of runners and joggers, whether the men are heart patients or men who run to avoid becoming heart patients are quite so generous as Mrs. Roberts; and Dr. Terence Kavanagh, alas, reports a few marital breakdowns from among the men in his group. There was the 36-year-old executive who hurried from the office to the track three evenings per week, then arrived home to "a wife who went out of her way to make him feel guilty because she couldn't accept that anything other than work would delay him from her." The couple separated. Even in the competitive world of track, marriages have split in two when wives have decided they were taking second place to running. Two long-distance runners from the 1968 US Olympic Team, for instance, continued to run after the Games but didn't continue to be married. And running cost three female middle-distance competitors from the 1972 US Olympic Team their husbands when the men walked, not ran, out of the marriages blaming the time devoted to track as the culprit.

The problem may not be so serious for conventional joggers, but jogging can still lay stresses and strains on marriages in which only one partner runs. Jealousy is the demon. "The situation gets especially acute," says psychologist Harrison Andover, "when a husband or wife takes up jogging after the marriage. If he or she has been doing if for years before marriage, then the non-running partner has already adjusted to it. But when it comes later, it's almost as if the husband or wife is having an affair. It *excludes* the person left at home."

Does Andover offer any advice to circumvent conflict?

"Sure. The jogger can help matters by breaking into the whole idea of jogging with a bit of finesse. He shouldn't suddenly start vanishing for a couple of hours at a time. He should discuss jogging with his wife, point out the benefits to his health and the benefits to her in having a healthy husband around the house. He should work his program into hours reasonably convenient to her. If possible, he could handle his jogging during noon hour when it wouldn't have any special impact on her. In cases where the jogger can see there's going to be a mild problem, he should use his noggin to keep the program as invisible and unobtrusive as he can. The same consideration applies to the jogging wife too.''

How about the spouse on the sidelines?

"Well," says Andover, "if the non-jogging partner is secure enough, then jogging presents no threat. But for wives or husbands who feel traces of resentment building inside them, I recommend that they develop some sort of activity or hobby, preferably physical, that they can put their energies to while their mates are out there jogging. That's one solution."

Is there another?

"There's the perfect solution."

Which is?

"The ones at home could take up jogging, too."

Dos and Don'ts

*Find your own jogging style: solo or social, each offers rewards.

*Jogging togetherness can rejuvenate family relationships.

*Don't let jogging crowd out the rest of your life.

Epilogue

*"I have only to think of putting on
my running shoes and the kinesthetic
pleasure of floating starts
to come over me."*
World marathon champion Ian Thompson

As I jogged on, around and
around the tiny oval track, beating out 24 laps to the mile, I
eventually stopped wondering about the value of what I was
doing. I found myself locked, unthinking, into my routine. I
didn't ask questions. I didn't bother to puzzle about the theo-
ries or philosophies behind jogging. I simply jogged. It was as
if I'd arrived at some variation on Descartes' dictum: *cogito,
ergo sum*. I perceive, therefore I am. How about *jogito, ergo
sum*? I jog, therefore I am. Silly, maybe, but true in my case.

And as I carried on, my old fear of the track began to fall
away. I was no longer reduced to the state of a quivering idiot

in the moments of dread anticipation before I started my workouts. My god, I *relished* them. I looked forward to my jogs, and that, for me, was a new and surprising attitude. My jogging diary, which I diligently maintained, began to reflect the changes that came over me. It grew from a glum monologue to something a good deal more optimistic, as the following few entries illustrate:

Day 41: Arrived in the gym feeling loggy. Not the result of any social excesses last night, just a general all-round case of the blahs. I went through my whole catalog of exercises anyway, and jogged a mile and three-quarters. And afterwards, to my astonishment, I felt sensationally satisfied. Somehow, from somewhere, my body responded, and I came out in a pleasantly tired and curiously refreshed condition. I was also minus the blahs.

Day 45: I notice that good joggers, the ones who move fastest and cover the most mileage, land with an almost noiseless tread. Bad joggers—well, bad in style—hit the track with heavy clumps. Sound, I realize, probably has little to do with the eventual benefits to one's cardiovascular system. Still, I think I'll concentrate on arriving at a silent step—I used to be a bit of a thumper—on the assumption that if I sound good, I'll feel good.

Day 52: My shins hurt. But I don't mind because they're the *only* part of me that hurts. Gradually, in the last week or so — this is the seventh week of my program — all the other bodily aches and torments have receded. Become non-existent, in fact. The pain in the shins occasionally snaps me with a sharp twinge or two, but so far it hasn't kept me off the track, and usually after I've covered ten or twelve laps, the soreness grows into a sort of companion, as natural a part of the jog as my shoes and shorts. Besides, it's glamorous to tell other people that I've got a case of shin splints. I mean, only Olympic athletes are supposed to come down with shin splints.

Day 55: I've edited my exercise program. Jettisoned most of the calisthenics and the routine on the stationary bike. I find them boring stuff, and once I hit the gym, I'm anxious to get on with the jog. So I've cut out everything except the warm-up and warm-down exercises. Wonder if Sam notices? Wonder if she thinks I'm cheating? Ah well, I rationalize in two ways: one, jogging is the most crucial, health-producing part of the program, and, two, the very fact that I'm keen to move straight to the jog must indicate that I'm getting hooked on it.

Day 60: Doing some fancy things to my jog. Like, instead of running three or four laps and then walking one, I'm going six or seven or eight laps, then a walk of one lap. I'm not forcing myself, mind you, not taking on the longer sessions unless I feel fresh to the attack. But the big distances—a quarter and a third of a mile at a chunk—seem to come naturally. A terrific sensation.

Day 63: Fanciest trick of all today. I ran for six laps on the heels of Reggie the Ghost. Don't know Reggie's last name. He's a kid in the early 20s who does four or five miles per day at a very fast clip, somewhere close to six minutes a mile I'd guess. And today, for the hell of it, I hung at his tail for six laps. Felt like I was challenging him for a gold medal. Pushing him to a world record. Forcing him to his limit. Landy against Bannister! Batten against Reggie the Ghost!

Day 67: Ran through the streets for the first time. Put on my track suit and slipped out under cover of darkness last night and jogged a mile and a half over a course through the neighborhood that I'd worked out earlier in the car. I jogged at night because I'm not quite ready to let the neighbors see me out of my civvies, but once I got into the jog, I felt perfectly relaxed. I discovered the need to keep a sharp eye on the ground that lies in my jogging path. At the track, I go on automatic pilot without worrying about obstacles. But on the sidewalks, I was wary of pedestrians, curbs, bicycles, parked cars and one dog (a barker but not a biter). Apart from that bother the jog was a glorious experience. Lots of passing urban scenery to keep the eyes busy, the cheer of the fresh air, the nice motion of feet passing over pavement. I also felt a snobbish sense of superiority when I looked in the windows of houses along the route, at the people inside hoisting drinks and watching television. *They* were going to seed. *I* was getting fit.

Day 72: Another first. I ran on grass and parkland. Went up to ravine and park near our house this afternoon and started to jog. I didn't have a special route or even a destination. I just took a couple of turns around the flat section of the park, then drifted down a hill to the bottom of the ravine and along a path that runs for part of its length. Some drawbacks, things like puddles (landed in two and came home with wet feet), tricky bits of terrain (almost turned my ankle in an invisible pothole), and occasional trouble with the wind (blown off course once), but mostly gratifying and fun. As I jogged, I felt a little as if I were taking something from nature, something damn near spiritual. There were the trees and the grass and the sky and then there was me, and we were together on a shared and secret little journey. Wow! Exhilaration!

Day 80: A game of squash today after six months away from the courts. The guy I played sticks at squash all year round. He won. "You're in good shape," he said to me afterwards. "In fact, you look like you could go another 20 minutes." Pause. "Too bad, I don't feel like that."

It was true — I'd arrived at something close to good shape. Or at any rate I was moving in that direction in ways that I, as well as my squash opponent, could begin to notice. At first, during the introductory five or six weeks of my jogging program, all I took note of was the pain of the process. I ached. The aches kept me from feeling any other sensation. And then this funny thing happened — I felt better, not by degrees but all at once. Was 'I undergoing the progression I'd read about in Kavanagh and Bowerman and in the other authoritative manuals? Reaching a plateau? I wasn't ready to swear it was so. I recognized, though, that I was running my distances more easily and finishing them less fatigued. I also recognized that the pains were fleeing, and as they left, I began to tick off the changes I noticed in my body and my life and my attitudes over the weeks that followed the dawning of the new me.

I had more stamina. For the last few years I'd made a ritual out of taking a nap for at least an hour every afternoon. I read somewhere that, shortly after Jack Kennedy's assassination, his widow advised the new president, Lyndon Johnson, to follow her late husband's example and nap each afternoon or he'd never find the energy to run the White House. If an afternoon rest was good enough for Kennedy and Johnson, I decided it was good enough for me. But once jogging took hold, I didn't need the nap. Instead of less energy, jogging gave me more. I typed and wrote and interviewed merrily through most afternoons, napless, without running out of steam. I found, though, that I couldn't get by on less sleep at night. I needed a solid eight hours. And I was getting them, a sounder sleep, the kind where you go out—click—like a light—within a few minutes of snapping out the real light beside the bed.

My sex life improved. I performed with more vigor and, ah, ... Well, let's draw the curtain on sex, leaving my wife and me cooing behind it, and move along to fish. Fish? Yes, I found myself eating more of it. I've always been partial to fish, but, post-jogging, I was more partial than usual. Should I attribute the increased affection for fish to jogging? For that matter, was jogging responsible for the stamina, the sounder sleep, the more vigorous sex? All I could be certain of was that the changes seemed to go hand-in-hand with the lengthening of my days and hours on the track. Jogging and the changes occurred, as they used to say in Richard Nixon's adminis-tration, at the same point in time. So did the differences in my attitude to food; I didn't consume more food but I consumed it with more relish. Although I put on two pounds, they were the result, I insisted, of fat giving way to hard muscle. Not all of these events could be marked down to coincidence. Jogging. I decided, deserved at least some credit.

At that point, I was deep into my third month of jogging, and I dared myself to take a couple of tests. First, the Kenneth Cooper 12-minute test. How much territory could I cover in 12 minutes? I realized that Cooper wants his followers to take the test close to the beginning of a fitness program, not 12 weeks into one, but — what the heck — I was using it as a special experiment. I took a stopwatch to a quarter-mile high-school track in our neighborhood. I chose it on the assumption, sensible I think, that all the turns on the 24-lap track where I regularly jogged wouldn't yield a fair reading.

I stepped on to the school track, snapped on the watch and set off around the quarter-mile layout. I jogged easily at first, speeded up after a half-mile, slowed to a near walk when I grew pooped at the mile mark, then put on a fresh burst of speed as the watch moved close to 12 minutes. The final whooshing drive got me around the track exactly six times. An even 1.5 miles in 12 minutes. I checked Cooper's chart: 1.5 to 1.74, I read, qualified for Category IV: Good. *Fantastic!* It was the first "Good" I'd scored in anything connected with fitness. True, 1.49 miles was only a whisper away and it qualified as Fair. If I hadn't run hard at the end, if I'd faltered by a few feet, then I would have found myself back in familiar territory, back in old Fair and Average. Still, I really had racked up 1.5 miles, and I'd take a Good any way it came.

Then I pronounced myself ready for the big test, the one that would once again put me head-to-head against the infernal 63-year-old Swede. Maximum Oxygen Uptake. This was the test, calculated by pedalling six or seven minutes on an ergometer while hooked up to an electro-cardiogram machine that measured efficiency in moving oxygen around the body. The more efficient the oxygen-transport system, the fitter the body. The ultimate test. Simple — except that the first time I'd taken the test, three months earlier, I registered a dreary 30, a figure that placed me in the category of Fair. It also placed me, at my age (44), two points behind the 63-year-old Swedish businessman, Bjorn Kjellstrom But that had been 12 weeks back. Had I changed in the meantime? Had jogging made a difference?

I turned once again to Sam. She — fit, smiling, gorgeous and concerned — buckled me into the ergometer and the EKG machine. I began pedalling. Sam monitored the machine. I pumped. She made silent notes. I pushed myself to the task. She moved easily between machine and notebook. It was over. I'd pedalled for seven minutes, and Sam had accumulated a lengthy catalog of data. She poured over it. I waited, more apprehensive than at any event except the birth of my first child, for the result of her calculations.

Hmmm, Sam murmured as she totted up numbers.

Please, I thought as I grew impatient, then nervous, then panicked.

"Thirty-seven," Sam said.

Thirty-seven. That marked me seven points up from my first score. According to Sam's charts for the Maximum Oxygen Uptake, 25-32 is Fair for my age, 33-39 is Average, 40-45 is

Good. I was Average, but I was in the upper reaches of Average. I was closing in on Good.

"Look at the improvement," Sam said. "Keep at your jogging."

She didn't need to tell me. I already knew that I had achieved my goal: I was more fit than the 65-year-old Swedish gentleman, even if he was really 63. The figures proved it. Dammit, I *was* getting fit.

For the first time since I started, I felt like an authentic jogger. One of the new breed.

Maximum Oxygen Uptake

Age Male	Excellent	Good	Average	Fair	Poor
20-29	54 +	53-45	44-40	39-33	32 −
30-39	50 +	49-43	42-35	34-27	26 −
40-49	46 +	45-40	39-33	32-25	24 −
50-59	44 +	43-38	37-31	30-22	21 −
60 +	40 +	39-35	34-29	28-21	20 −
Female					
20-29	50 +	48-44	43-35	34-29	28 −
30-39	46 +	45-41	40-34	33-28	27 −
40-49	42 +	41-37	36-30	29-24	23 −
50 +	38 +	37-32	32-27	26-21	20 −

A Selected Bibliography of Books About Running and Jogging

Cooper, Kenneth, *The New Aerobics*. (1970, M. Evans).
    Aerobics. (1968, M. Evans).
Cooper, Kenneth and Mildred Cooper. *Aerobics for Women*. (1973, Bantam).
Glasser, William. *Positive Addiction*. (1976, Harper and Row).
Harris, W.E. *Jogging: A Complete Physical Fitness Program for All Ages*. (1967, Grosset & Dunlap).
Henderson, Joe. *The Long-Run Solution*. (1976, World Pubns.).
        Run Gently, Run Long. (1976, World Pubns.).
Runner's World Editors.
    The Complete Runner. (1975, World Pubns.).
    Beginning Running. (1972, World Pubns.).
Sheehan, George. *Doctor Sheehan on Running*. (1976, World Pubns.).
Ullyot, Joan. *Women's Running*. (1976, World Pubns.).
Van Aaken, Ernst. *The Van Aaken Method: Finding the Endurance to Run Faster and Live Healthier*. (1976, World Pubns.).